SIMPLE.
PRACTICAL.
EFFECTIVE.

A Framework for Literacy-Focused Instructional Leadership
High School Edition

Dr. Marquis S. Dwarte

Copyright © 2020 by Dr. Marquis Dwarte

All rights reserved. No parts of this book may be used or reproduced in any manner whatsoever without the express written permission of the publisher except for the use of brief quotations in a book review.

Printed in the United States of America

ISBN: 978-1-7358701-0-6

ISBN: 978-1-7358701-1-3 (ebook)

First printing, 2020

JayMedia Publishing

Laurel MD 20708

www.publishing.jaymediagroup.net

DEDICATION

This book is dedicated to my daughter, Kylie Arianna Dwarte, who since the day she was born has served as my greatest source of purpose, inspiration, motivation, and strength. Kylie, you are my world!

ACKNOWLEDGEMENTS

During my life, I have been fortunate to have benefited from great support, counsel, and mentorship from a cross-section of people. While the number of people who have aided in my life's accomplishments is innumerable, there are several key figures whom I would be remiss in failing to acknowledge.

First and foremost, I would like to acknowledge my parents, Mark and Deborah Dwarte, for their unconditional support of my ambitions. Since the day I was born, they have made countless sacrifices in an effort to position me for success. They taught me the value of discipline, dedication, and determination. For that, I will forever be grateful. I would also like to acknowledge my "big sis," Chenee, who has been a life mentor.

Second, I would like to acknowledge several key mentors who have been instrumental in guiding me and nurturing my maturation as an educator and as a leader. To Pat, Louis, Buddy, Monique, Brian, and Deborah, words cannot express how thankful I have been over the years for your support and guidance through the highs and lows of my career. Whenever I called, you answered, and that means a lot to me.

Last, I would like to sincerely thank all of those whom I have had the fortune of working with during my journey as an educator. In particular, I would like to give a shout out to the staffs of IA and OHS for the good work we did together and thank them for fully embracing me as their principal. It is also important that I specifically acknowledge the contributions Leah made to the development of the ACE program that is described in chapter 7 of this book.

TABLE OF CONTENTS

INTRODUCTION

Aims and Intents ix

Part I: GETTING STARTED

Chapter 1: The Leadership Imperative 3
Chapter 2: The "Core Four" 9

Part II: LITERACY LEADERSHIP

Chapter 3: Instructional Leadership in Action 17
Chapter 4: Leveraging Literacy 23
Chapter 5: Supporting Literacy-Focused Instruction 37

Part III: ACTION PLANNING

Chapter 6: Strategic Planning for College and Career Readiness 51
Chapter 7: Effective Middle to High School Transition 53
Chapter 8: The College Metrics 69
Chapter 9: Fulfilling the "Promise of Preparation" 81

Part IV: CONCLUSION

Chapter 10: Final Thoughts 93

INTRODUCTION

Aims and Intents

As one ascends to the role of school leader, he or she is entrusted with the safety and emotional well-being of hundreds or even thousands of students. Subsequently, the educator is thrust into a "political" position of high visibility and expected to understand and respond to the broader community needs. He or she is expected to operate a multi-million dollar physical plant and assume fiduciary responsibilities over hundreds of thousands of taxpayers' dollars while providing supervision for staff ranging from teachers to counselors, to administrative assistants, to custodians, and cafeteria workers. This is all on top of assuming a school leader's primary role of being the "instructional leader," evaluated principally by the capacity to improve learning for every student in all subjects. When expressed in this context, most would concur that such a high-stakes, demanding, and expansive role could only be perceived as daunting.

This is what happens every year when thousands of superintendents and their local school boards approve thousands of school leaders' promotions. The promotion from teacher to assistant principal or assistant principal to principal is no small feat, and with this new title comes unnerving yet exciting challenges. The emotional and physical tolls exacted on those in school leadership positions are rivaled in few other professions. Being charged with educating people's most prized possessions, their children, and assuming the bulk of the responsibility for preparing tomorrow's workforce offers little margin for error. While school leaders' roles appear to pose impossible odds, those who approach the job with a clear purpose, the right people, and well-crafted plans can achieve success even considering such odds. Firsthand, I can tell you that there is no greater professional fulfillment than being at the helm of a school where the staff is thriving and students are highly supported in their quest for learning.

Thus, there is a double intention for writing this book. This book's primary focus is to detail the process by which secondary school educators can leverage literacy to improve learning and ensure students are truly prepared for college and careers. To that end, parts II and III of the book will feature a series of well-designed and coherent plans that can aid school leaders in framing their approach to action planning in the name of school improvement. Sample plans for several key initiatives and focuses at the high school level will be presented. The common thread in each of these initiatives and their corresponding action plans will be literacy and how it can be harnessed as the single most powerful tool in driving notable achievement and preparing students for life beyond K-12 school.

However, it would be ill-advised for any book on school leadership not to address leadership more holistically. Part I of this book begins with discussing the nuances, complexities, and opportunities encountered by school leaders as they confront the challenges of leading teachers and improving learning outcomes for all students. To understand school improvement, one must first understand those leadership characteristics and factors that transcend leadership in any field, industry, or organization. These characteristics and factors must then be applied in the context of school leadership, thereby ensuring an operational understanding of "instructional leadership." In other words, effective school leaders need to understand how to integrate leadership in a broad context with a keen sense of how to support improved pedagogy anchored in literacy. This book aims to provide that understanding as well as resources for those interested in improving outcomes for students.

For the most part, those reading this book will likely fall into one of two categories: those who are working to develop a clear plan for instructional improvement and those who have already done so. It is my hope that those in the former category will take away a better understanding of school leadership and school improvement. For those who fall into the latter category, the hope is that this book extends your learning and serves as an affirmation of the work you have done. Whatever the case, I hope you find the book to be instructive and useful. The material presented in this book is simple, practical, and effective.

Part I
GETTING STARTED

CHAPTER 1

The Leadership Imperative

Leadership – The Challenges that Lie Ahead for School Leaders

School-based leadership, namely, the role of principal, poses a uniqueness that is rivaled in few careers. School leaders are tasked with a litany of responsibilities and must work effectively with a multitude of constituents ranging from district leadership to parents, to students, to community stakeholders who represent an array of divergent interests. On any given school day, school leaders can be tasked with intervening in student confrontations, responding to major community issues, working with teachers to improve pedagogy, writing compliance reports, managing budgetary expenditures, meeting with concerned groups of parents and other stakeholder groups, and an exhaustive list of other tasks necessary for the efficient and effective operation of a school. Couple this list of responsibilities with levels of accountability that far exceed those of most other professions, and you have a perfect storm of challenges. The aggregation of stringent accountability, as well as the scope of responsibility associated with the role of a principal, have effectively created an executive-level position that is often viewed as overwhelming.

The work that school leaders do is complex in that the metrics for effectiveness vary widely, and these leaders are accountable to an array of constituents, most of whom have a very different, and sometimes ignorant, view of the position. Unlike business industries, there is simply not a bottom line that one can outline to gauge your effectiveness. Rather, amongst other things, school leaders' effectiveness depends on school culture, academic achievement, community trust, parent satisfaction, community partnerships, the hiring and retention of quality teachers and educators, fiscal responsibility, the safety of students, and, in the age of accountability, the "all-important" test scores. As a high school principal, these tests scores often encompass students' performances on state-mandated tests as well as measures of college readiness, including graduation rates, performance on the SAT or ACT, as well as pass rates on Advanced Placement (AP) and International Baccalaureate (IB) exams. This level of job complexity gives way to the following facts and statistics:

According to MetLife (2012):

- Three-quarters (75%) of principals feel the job has become too complex
- Job satisfaction among principals has decreased nine percentage points in less than five years, to 59% very satisfied down from 68% very satisfied in 2008
- Half (48%) of principals experience great stress several days a week

Further, results from the 2017 Principal Health and Wellbeing Survey revealed:

- Half of principals have faced threats of violence at work
- One in three experienced actual violence
- Half of all principals worked 56 hours a week, 27% worked up to 65 hours a week
- Principals reported higher levels of burnout than the general population, twice as much difficulty sleeping as a result of stress, and were at higher risk for depression
- Principals said red tape and the increasing accountability requirements demanded by governments were hindering teaching and learning in the classroom

Finally, according to the 2018 Principal Occupational Health, Safety, and Wellbeing Survey:

When compared to the general population, principals have:

- 1.5 times higher job demands
- 1.6 times more burnout

- 1.7 times more stress
- 2.2 times more difficulty sleeping
- 1.3 times more depressive symptoms

Amidst the ever-changing landscape of education and in light of the ever-increasing demands on school leaders, the need for effective school leadership remains constant. As I write this book, there is, once again, a major and dramatic shift in education policies. During the past several years, school leaders have been charged with the ushering in of a barrage of reforms including: a new approach to teacher and principal evaluation, the implementation of the common core curriculum and related assessments, a rethinking of the way we approach teaching and learning, a new accountability system designed to produce evidence of students' readiness for college and the workforce, and the demand for school leaders to help communities navigate increasingly complex equity issues. As a result, some would argue that the changes associated with the Every Student Succeeds Acts (ESSA) are more complex and robust than past reforms, including the Elementary and Secondary Education Act of 1965 and its 2001 reauthorization, better known as "No Child Left Behind." At the helm of our Nation's schools, through these unprecedented changes, are and will continue to be our school leaders. This is a challenging time for education leaders as accountability has increased dramatically, and school leaders, for the most part, will inherit many of the challenges and burdens associated with the "era of education accountability."

Leadership - The Stakes

Having spent the bulk of my educational career in the ranks of school-based leadership, I have developed a deep appreciation for the challenging and vital work that school leaders do each day to improve students' lives and school communities as a whole. I am confident we can agree that educators, outside of our servicemen and servicewomen in the military, are among the most essential professionals in our Nation. Our freedom, democracy, and overall well-being as a nation of people are contingent upon educated and well-informed citizens. Education serves as the leading platform for ensuring our citizens can meet the academic, career, social, and cultural demands necessary for our country to continue thriving as a beacon of prosperity and freedom. Every outstanding achievement and advancement was made possible and underwritten by teachers and the schooling process. Without great teachers led by exceptional school leaders, there would have been no industrial revolution, no man on the moon, no globalization via the internet. Teaching and learning have propelled us from the "Stone Age" to the most advanced country the world has ever known.

Thus, the stakes could not be higher than they are for school leaders; the charge is exact, and the purpose is without rival in terms of significance. As education goes, so, too, does a society. This notion serves to buttress the critical role of school leaders. School leaders must be chief executive officers, teachers, coaches, mentors, community ambassadors, and a litany of other things. To be effective, the school leader must be able to, with great fluidity, move between these roles as dictated by various situations and circumstances. The challenge is both inspiring and daunting, but it is far from impossible as long as school leaders have proper guidance and a clear understanding of the roles simplicity and practicality play in effective instructional leadership.

Leadership - Less is More

Those of us who study or work in the social sciences, whether it be fields like education or politics, have often been subjected to long-winded, cumbersome, and overly convoluted policies or improvement plans. These documents are crafted with the intent of molding positive changes. Still, many times the content of such plans relies on theory or extensive ideas that do not approximate the realities of what can be done and how it can be done. These plans lack the simplicity and practicality needed to be understood and fully actualized.

A professor and mentor of mine once remarked, "If I had more time, I would have written a shorter dissertation." As an early career educator in one of my first doctoral-level courses, I was unable to grasp the point he was making. In all honesty, I ignored his point and maintained my belief that lengthy and complex writings and plans were essential to making marked improvement, whether in the field of education or otherwise. I would surmise with a great degree of certainty that I was not alone in my thinking at that time. It was not until years later, as I progressed further into my career as a leader in the field of education, that his remarks resonated with me. The essence of what he said was that it is easy to communicate your ideas in lengthy, complex documents and plans, but the real work in helping people to make meaning of your ideas lies in your ability to achieve brevity and simplicity. His point gives way to a quote by Albert Einstein, who said, "Any intelligent fool can make things bigger and more complex. It takes a touch of genius - and a lot of courage - to move in the opposite direction." Here, we have a highly educated professor coupled with one of the greatest minds the world has ever known, making a similar point. That is, brevity and simplicity are among the truest indicators of how well an idea, plan, or strategy can be communicated and, more importantly, understood. Yet, far too many leaders across industries fail to take heed to this uncomplicated fact and thereby work to create systems, structures, and processes that are so complex they are unable to be effectively implemented neither at full scale nor within certain segments of the organization. The idea of simplicity being a key factor in organizational success is a concept that is "so simple, it's complex."

As a school leader, you will work with people representing a wide mix of interests and personalities and with varying abilities. It is the leader who cannot only formulate a vision, mission, and goals but can also develop plans and processes that are clear, concise, and simple, who will most likely achieve success for one's school. Most people, inherently, crave simplicity and clear direction for what they are being asked to do. Educators are no different. Thus, the primary goal of this book is to provide education leaders with an easily understood framework and practical resources that will ensure success even in the face of stiffening odds.

SUMMARY

So, given the challenges outlined, how do school leaders provide effective leadership?

As a football coach and player, I heard many profound quotes and sound bites, but none rings truer than what my high school coach used to say about the game of football. In his mind, the team that had the players who blocked and tackled the best would far more often than not win the game. For those non-football fans, the essence of his statement was rooted in the premise that the most basic fundamentals of the sport frequently determined the outcome of games. It was not until I became a school principal charged with managing the implementation of a multitude of what I saw as disjointed, "flavor of the week" programs and district initiatives that his quote began to resonate with me. In essence, his quote was based on the power of focusing on core factors (some would say fundamentals) that, while they seem to be rudimentary, are enduring, everlasting, and for which there are no substitutions. Relative to football, no matter how intricate your schemes are, if you do not block or tackle well, your schemes will be futile. The most effective leaders are committed to the fundamentals because these fundamentals are timeless and, when done well, always bear positive results.

As I introduce these fundamental leadership themes, a natural inclination will likely be to remark about their simplistic and practical nature, but you may be surprised by the number of leaders who cannot articulate the value of using these themes to guide their actions. Further, many of these same leaders fail to recognize the synergistic nature of these themes. I believe that this is largely due to the fact that as educators, we are constantly at the mercy of policy changes and often find ourselves bogged down in managing an overwhelming number of programs, models, and initiatives. As a consequence, school leaders sometimes struggle because they get caught in the weeds; they become heavily reliant on being reactive and lose sight of the importance of their people, having a purpose, developing and vetting a plan, and the need for commitment and persistence. These themes keep leaders focused and prepared and position them for success.

Chapter 2 of the book will present and describe the fundamentals of leadership referenced as the "Core Four" and how success as a leader begins first with getting to the core.

CHAPTER 2

The "Core Four"

The Core Four

As mentioned, I have spent the past two decades working in education, and my experiences have spanned the entire K-16 continuum. Thus, I have been fortunate enough to collect a series of experiences that I believe to be essential for effective school leadership. Through my years of experience as a teacher, coach, counselor, principal, and senior-level district administrator, I have developed an appreciation for highly effective leaders. I have spent a great deal of time and energy attempting to understand what it takes to be a highly effective leader in the field of education. In both my academic research on this topic as well as my own personal anecdotes, four themes have continued to emerge. I believe these themes act as the "core" of leadership. They are "people," "purpose," "plan," and "persistence."

A more nuanced understanding of what I call the "core" or "core four" is required to tackle the challenges of school leadership. To get to the "core," leaders must steer clear of those extraneous distracters that too often result in leaders "taking their eyes off the ball" in pursuit of novelty and complexity rather than proven and simple approaches. Leaders, more so than anyone else, must be obsessive about "keeping their eyes on the ball" at all costs. In many instances, highly effective leaders understand these four factors, and they focus their efforts, time, and energy on them. To that end, let's briefly explore the core four:

1. People - They Matter
2. Purpose - Must be Clear
3. Plan - Has to be Focused, Aligned, and Simple
4. Persistence - Trust the Process

CORE #1: People - They Matter

During his presidential campaigns in the early 1990s, William "Bill" Clinton summed up the necessities of the country and its people with the expression "It's the economy, stupid." President Clinton was merely noting that addressing the economic needs of the people was the foundation and impetus for all other policy matters and for improving the lives of the American people. For education leaders, I believe attracting and retaining the right people is as critical to your success as a leader as the third leg of a stool is to its functionality. Success as a school leader is first and foremost about the people surrounding you. Simply put, not having the right people will render even the best plans and strategies meaningless (Whitaker, 2009). As a caution, please do not conflate the right people with the brightest people because those two things are not synonymous and are sometimes mutually exclusive (Colvin, 2010).

I have spent a great deal of time reading books and attending conferences and workshops where presenters discuss some detailed school improvement plan or instructional leadership model that is being promulgated as a panacea for school performance. Yet, they seldom reference the pivotal role people play in executing these plans. At this point, these models and the people who purport them fluctuate between laughably amusing and ignorantly offensive. Any leader worth one's salt should know that all great accomplishments start first with the "who," meaning the people who are at the ground level and who are expected to execute the plan. Losing sight of the importance of "getting the right people on the bus" (à la Jim Collins) is a recipe for nothingness at best and disaster at worst.

CORE #2: Purpose - Must be Clear and Compelling

There is nothing worse than a leader who cannot evoke a clear sense of purpose in those he or she is charged with leading. Providing clarity of the "purpose" is undoubtedly a critical aspect of leadership. In essence, by giving those you lead a clear sense of purpose, you are reinforcing the "why" behind your plan and essentially all the work to which you are asking them to commit.

When I reflect on all the leaders with whom I have had an association, whether in a professional setting or on the playing field, one of the biggest factors distinguishing those whom I perceived as effective versus ineffective was their ability to clearly communicate a sense of purpose that resonated with members of the team or organization. To me, clarity of purpose reinforces the value of the work that the staff is embarking upon.

To establish a clear purpose a leader has to set worthwhile, audacious goals tightly aligned to the organization's beliefs and values. Furthermore, these goals must be meaningful and grounded in pushing everyone to be their very best. While the importance of having the right people cannot be underscored enough, it is the purpose that is the impetus, the "rallying cry," that unites and mobilizes everyone around common goals. By establishing a clear and compelling purpose, effective leaders are able to harness people's passions and talents in such a way that there is an unwavering belief that bold goals can and will be accomplished. Having a clear purpose must be a foremost priority for all leaders irrespective of their chosen profession.

CORE #3: Plan - Has to be Focused, Aligned, and Simple

Once armed with the right people (the "who") as well as a clear and compelling purpose (the "why"), the leader is now ready to lay out the plan and strategies (the "how") for improving and attaining organizational goals. While the people and purpose are significant in their own rights, so, too, is the plan. Without a thoughtfully crafted plan, you are left with a group of the right people motivated by a compelling purpose, but their enthusiasm and commitment will quickly wane if they are not supported and guided by a plan for moving forward. The plan is essentially your guide, your map, your game plan. A good coach would not fathom putting his or her team on the field without a game plan, and an effective school leader would never think of not having an improvement plan that provides clear direction. In short, without a plan for achieving your goals, you are wasting everyone else's time and efforts; this will soon morph into frustration and burnout.

While people are inspired by bold and complex goals, they, contrarily, yearn for simplicity in the approach to reaching those goals. Despite this notion, many leaders remain drawn to complexity which, in turn, leads to convolution and misguided actions. To buttress this point, Mike Schmoker (2011) noted in his book, *Focus,* far too often, leaders become enamored with novelty and quick-fix solutions that are often unproven, complex, cumbersome, and simply unsustainable. And, for those noted reasons, these novel ideas and programs, at best, give an illusion, a mirage of sorts, that true improvement is being achieved. At worst, these ideas and programs cause confusion, dysfunction, and undermine meaningful improvement. There are two lessons here. First, if you are intent on being a successful leader, you must have a plan, and it better be a damn good one. Second, effective leaders know how to keep things simple.

Core #4: Persistence - Trust the Process

As the famed author Jim Collins (2001) remarked in his renowned book, *Good to Great*, most people and organizations are undisciplined. In my experience, this statement rings true on many levels. In many cases, staff members are often on board with the vision, purpose, and plan devised to affect improvement. However, it is the lack of will to carry out the plan with fierce diligence that inhibits an organization's success. This is often a function of people's natural propensity to stray away from intended goals and performance plans, especially when success is not achieved with immediacy. Confronted with the reality that there will be a need for prolonged efforts and unwavering discipline, far too many people waiver and succumb to disbelief in their plan and in the process. Meaningful improvement requires more than plans and strategies; it requires sustained commitment and sound execution. Like therapy or drugs taken for medicinal purposes, plans and strategies aimed at improving necessitate time to get into the system and take hold. Achieving success requires a commitment to and devout trust in the process.

To ensure persistence, leaders must inspire others to "ignore the noise" and to maintain focus on their commitment to the sound implementation of the plan. Leaders must, at all costs, stay disciplined, and keep those whom they lead disciplined as well. Remaining disciplined requires determination and confidence that the plan, executed over time and with the proper support, will drive the organization to its intended goals. The best leaders remain resolute in their discipline and commitment to the plan, and they model this behavior in their actions and in their messaging. Keeping people focused and on message requires intentional consistency in actions and in communication. Effective leaders know their behaviors and words have consequences and, thus, they keep everyone focused by their strict adherence to staying on message.

SUMMARY

The noted "core four" areas are all requisites for effective leadership, and all four must be effectively accounted for when endeavoring to achieve success as an instructional leader. However, leaders tend to fall short in their ability to successfully devise effectual plans. This inability can be incapacitating in that even when the "right people are in place," the "purpose is clear," and there is a "willingness to persist," the probability of finding success in the absence of the "right plan" is low. Put in a more practical context, even the most talented and dedicated group of individuals in any sector or organization will fall short of achieving their goals in the absence of a well-devised and well-orchestrated plan.

The plan is the road map that guides all decisions made and efforts undertaken; it is the bridge that connects where you are as an organization to where you want or need to be. Leaders without the right plan set people on a course to wander aimlessly in the dark and with no compass. Improvement planning in the context of instructional leadership is the foremost imperative when attempting to improve school performance. As such, Part II of this book focuses exclusively on devising "the plan," that constitutes sound instructional leadership driven by the most critical and time-tested variable associated with school improvement, which is literacy. This is achieved by connecting literacy-focused instructional leadership as "the plan" to college and career readiness as "the purpose," and by offering a practical framework as well as resources for doing so.

Part II
LITERACY LEADERSHIP

CHAPTER 3

Instructional Leadership in Action

Operationalizing Instructional Leadership

Those who work in the field of education are aware of the ever-expanding list of jargon used to highlight important aspects of an educator's work. At best, these jargon terms are loosely defined, and at worst, they serve as the basis for confusion among educators leading to a lack of true understanding. Educators have become accustomed to citing and discussing these terms while not fully comprehending their aims and intents.

A simple Google search of terms like "rigor," "engagement," "data-driven," "best practices," "critical thinking," "student-centered," "equity," and "instructional leadership" will serve only to offer more confusion as definitions, understandings, and interpretations of these words vary drastically and lack consistency. Yet, it is unlikely that one can find an educator who has attended any staff or collaborative planning meeting, sat in any conference session, or read any education-related article that does not reference these or some of the many other jargon terms which we have become so accustomed to hearing. Nonetheless, there remains no consensus on what these terms truly mean. In the education leadership circles, there are few terms more commonly mentioned than "instructional leadership." The expansive use of this term is far-reaching, but its definition remains evasive, and many educators struggle to pinpoint what instructional leadership is and what an instructional leader does.

In the research sciences, vague, widely defined terms and ideas, like those mentioned above, are referred to as "broad constructs," which are open to interpretation and misunderstanding. It is not until these broad constructs are "operationalized" that true clarity and uniformity in understanding is evoked. To operationalize a word, term, or concept, one needs to define how it is observed and measured. Being able to observe and measure something makes it tangible and, thus, more precisely understood. It is with this clarity of understanding that systems, structures, and processes can be devised to enact improvement. School leaders must carefully spell out the terms of their "purpose" and their "plans." This is the first step toward instructional leadership.

In an effort to distill instructional leadership down to a clear definition I offer the following. Instructional leadership is about (a) establishing a clear purpose, (b) setting meaningful and clear-cut academic goals, (c) developing and implementing well-thought plans for achieving these goals, and (d) building systems to monitor progress toward these goals. The effective instructional leader understands this and can, with ease, articulate all four of those prior points. In the end, instructional leadership is about having the right academic goals and the right instructional plan. While this definition may seem overly simplistic and mundane, it truly is the foundation of sound instructional leadership.

Effective Instructional Leadership

In my experience, principals who have been the most successful in shaping and driving improvement as "instructional leaders" are those who harness the core four ("people," "purpose," "plan," and "persistence") while incessantly understanding that the plan must be clear, simple, and easily executed. Knowing that the plan is the foremost element to success, the effective instructional leader must facilitate the development of a plan that is focused on driving improvements in student learning (Whitaker, 2018). To do this, one must first establish quantitative goals that serve as markers or indicators for progress toward the broader "purpose." With those goals in mind, the leader must then create a straightforward pathway, "the plan," for reaching the stated goals. The pathway is then operationalized as a series of measurable strategies and actions. Following this process is the essence of "backward mapping." You start first with the "purpose" and goals as the "destination," establish checkpoints as "markers," and then make certain that you have a clear plan as the pathway for reaching your destination and in, more specifically, achieving your goals. Figure 1 illustrates the prior points in a conceptual manner.

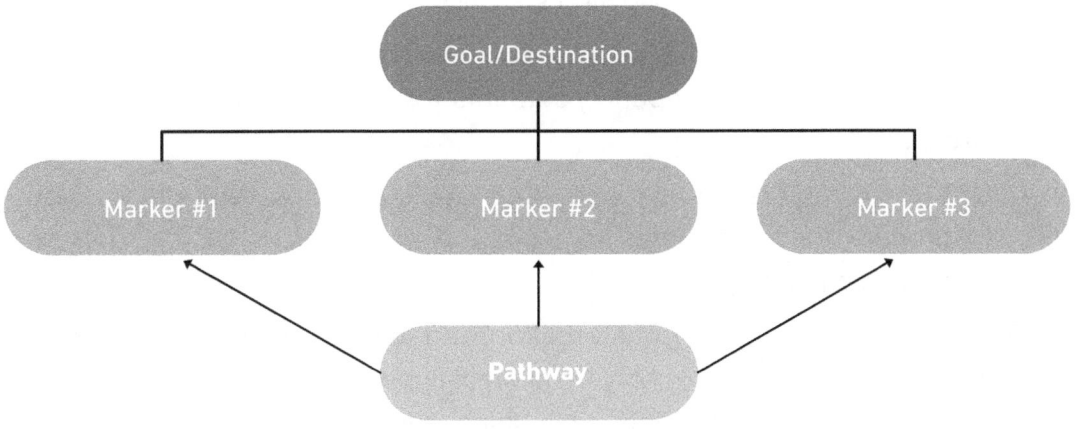

Figure 1: ***The Pathway***

True Readiness as "The Purpose"

For generations, a high school diploma essentially punched one's ticket to middle-class life. Armed with a college degree one could certainly expect to live among the upper-middle class. Unfortunately, this is not the reality of contemporary generations. Now, it is imperative that schools, especially high schools, create a pathway to ensuring students are well-prepared to excel in their post-secondary endeavors. As a result, in recent years, the focal point of the conversation regarding the principal purpose of high schools has shifted from a push for college and career eligibility to a more pronounced focus on college and career readiness (CCR). The semantic variation in these two terms, eligible comparative to readiness, may seem subtle. However, the ramifications of their deeper, implicit differences are considerable.

No longer is it acceptable for schools and school systems to perceive their main purpose as simply ensuring students graduate high school. While this narrow focus has been the case for decades, the new-age, globalized economy demands a more competitive high school graduate; this means a graduate who is more than merely eligible for a job or for enrollment at an institute of higher learning, but one who can compete for gainful employment and college acceptance with their cohorts from around the globe. The focus on eligibility versus true readiness has resulted in staggering college attrition rates as well as employers' disdain regarding recent high school graduates' readiness to assume entry-level positions in the workforce. More specifically, nearly 40% of all college enrollees fail to complete college within six years (U.S. Department of Education, 2019). To further drive home this point, consider the following statistics:

- 78% of college instructors report that public high schools aren't doing a good enough job of preparing students for college coursework (Achieve. Org, n.d.)
- 62% of employers surveyed say that public schools aren't doing enough to prepare their graduates to meet the expectations of the workplace (Achieve.Org, n.d.)

These data are causes for consternation, and to not take aim at preparing our students for success would not only be malfeasance, but it would also be dangerous to the future of our students' well-being and our standing as the world's economic power.

When presented with these alarming data, the question then becomes, What factor is contributing most to the lack of academic skills among many of America's contemporary high school graduates? To answer this question, one only needs to cite the decline in literacy levels in America's K-12 schools. The Alliance for Excellent Education (2016) highlighted the following facts with regards to adolescent literacy: (a) more than 60% of 8th graders and 60% of 12th graders scored below the proficient level on the most recent administration of the National Assessment of Education Progress (NAEP), (b) overall, 29% of 12th graders scored below the basic level, and (c) only 20% of students meeting the criteria for low-income status scored at or above the proficient level. Further, when assessing workforce preparedness levels of recent high school graduates, it was reported that 61% of employers require additional training and education in the areas of reading and writing for these entry-level employees.

These low literacy levels provide a better understanding of where the breakdown in preparing American students to excel in college and in the workforce rests (Gallagher, 2009). Essentially, we have a pervasive literacy issue which, left unchecked, will serve only to accelerate and exacerbate the unpreparedness of many of today's students. So, if we understand that our collective goal as educators is to ensure college and workforce readiness, then my subsequent proclamation should resonate. If the destination (purpose and goals) is true college and workforce readiness, then the plan (pathway) must be deeply rooted in literacy.

Any attempt to improve college and workforce readiness without absolute regard for literacy is a surefire plan for failure in achieving this paramount goal. Consequently, I insistently urge that instructional leaders adopt literacy as the pathway to achieving college and career readiness for all of their students. The power of improved literacy is unquestioned. It is our best defense against the lack of readiness affecting our graduates, and it provides us protection from the inequalities and subsequent inequities that continue to plague American schools. As a principal, I once told my staff, "Show me a failing school, and I will show you a school where the overwhelming majority of students struggle to read and write." With that in mind, the following figure extends and applies more specificity to what was shown in Figure 1.

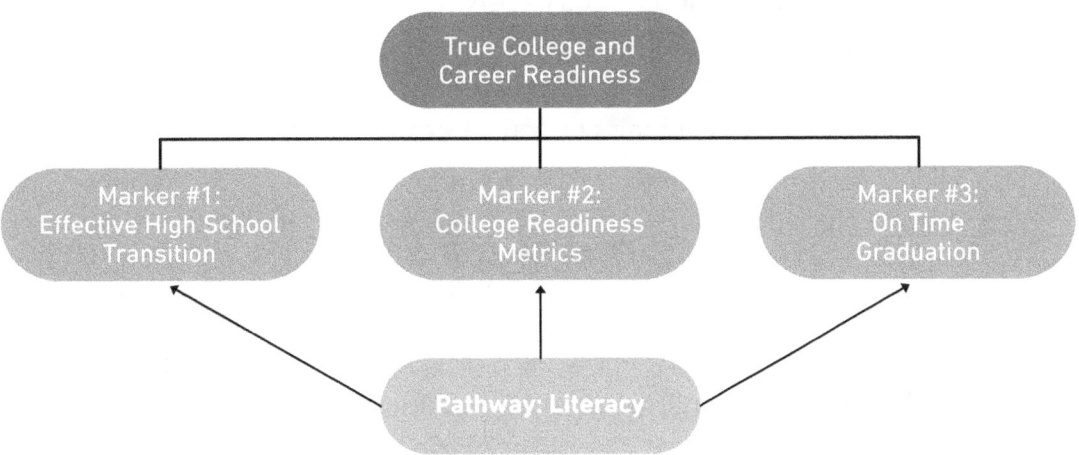

Figure 2: *A Pathway to College and Career Readiness*

As shown in Figure 2, improved CCR is greatly dependent upon a plan that takes aim at improving literacy as its pathway. Among the primary indicators of improved college and career readiness are:

1. **Effective Middle School to High School Transitions**: Failure to give careful attention to this transition places high schools and their students at an immediate disadvantage. This is a school's first opportunity to begin the process of building and refining literacy skills, as well as other important soft skills, of their students. The importance of focusing on literacy as a key component of this transition cannot be overemphasized.

2. **Performance on College Metrics**: Now, these metrics vary from system to system and state to state. However, by and large, they are represented by a combination of several critical assessments. These include performance

on cumulative assessments, including the SAT or the ACT. Also included in the suite of college metrics is performance on program-related course assessments, whether they be for the Advanced Placement program (AP) or International Baccalaureate program (IB). Both of these assessments provide an objective gauge of students' readiness for college work and with regard to the academic skills needed to find early career success. Further, exposure to and performance on these metrics are, oftentimes, important factors in the college admissions process.

3. **On-Time Graduation**: Above all else, schools must exhaust their efforts to ensure students graduate high school on time and equipped with the literacy skills needed to function as well-informed citizens. This includes the ability to read, write, and discuss everyday issues that impact their lives. It also includes their ability to read, write, speak and listen at a level and in a manner that ensures they can acquire and communicate the information required for success in their chosen career.

SUMMARY

By applying this conceptual framework, high school leaders will be well on their way to leveraging "instructional leadership" as the means to improving readiness levels for the students they serve. So, the effective instructional leader knows and understands the core four and sets goals that best ensure students are poised to graduate from high school truly ready for colleges, careers, and society. In the end, effective "instructional leadership" starts down a pathway forged by literacy and grounded in preparing students to excel in life beyond high school.

CHAPTER 4

Leveraging Literacy

Literacy as "The Plan & Pathway"

As an instructional leader, it is incumbent upon you to start first by focusing your plan on those instructional areas that are essential to student engagement, student learning, and ultimately, school improvement. Regarding the true essence of teaching and learning, there is no better focus than that of one grounded in literacy. The power of literacy is almost immeasurable as it impacts every content area and every aspect of one's life starting in the earliest stages of childhood and increasing in importance as we age. Literacy is often misperceived as referencing only reading, but literacy includes not only one's ability to read but also a person's ability to organize information, to speak, to listen, to discuss, and to write. When one can read, discuss, and write extensively about a topic, then he or she has likely achieved the ability to think critically about the topic at hand. As an effective instructional leader, you would be well-advised to ensure that literacy is a focal point of your teaching expectations and your staff development. While literacy has traditionally been believed to be an area most important to elementary schools, it is just as important, if not more so, to secondary level students. Yet, we often lose sight of the purpose and value of literacy as students matriculate through K-12 schooling. While literacy may certainly look different at each level of schooling, it is imperative that school leaders not lose sight of its importance and instead place it as the "centerpiece" of teaching and learning. If you remain unconvinced about the power of literacy and the pivotal role it plays in quality education, its impact in terms of equity, and how it sets the foundation for college and career readiness, then please carefully consider the following:

The Literacy Project, an organization focused on advancing literacy efforts across the United States, aggregated and highlighted research from sources including the National Institute for Literacy, National Center for Adult Literacy, The Literacy Company, and U.S. Census Bureau. In doing so, they revealed the succeeding statistics as they relate to the crucial role that literacy plays in success in school and in life:

General:

- Currently, 45 million Americans are functionally illiterate and cannot read above a fifth-grade level
- Fifty percent of adults cannot read a book written at an eighth-grade level
- One-third of fourth-graders reach the proficient reading level
- Eighty-five percent of juvenile offenders have problems reading
- Three out of five people in American prisons cannot read
- Three out of four people on welfare cannot read

Literacy Development:

- According to the Department of Education, the more students read or are read to for fun on their own time and at home, the higher their reading scores.
- Reading and being read aloud to has an impact that extends beyond just hearing stories; it builds one's vocabulary, thereby ensuring higher comprehension levels.
- In a study of nearly 100,000 U.S. school children, access to printed materials was the key variable affecting reading acquisition.
- Books for kids contain 50% more words than children are likely to encounter in regular conversation, TV, or radio.
- Higher reading exposure was 95% positively correlated with a growing region supporting semantic language processing in the brain.

Social and Cultural:

- In middle-income neighborhoods, the ratio of books per child is 13 to 1; in low-income neighborhoods, the ratio is one age-appropriate book for every 300 children.

- Sixty-one percent of low-income families have no books at all in their homes for their children.
- Thirty-seven percent of children arrive at kindergarten without the literacy skills necessary for lifetime learning.
- Fifty percent of children from low-income communities start first grade up to two years behind their peers.
- One in four children in America grow up without learning how to read.
- A child is 90% likely to remain a poor reader at the end of the fourth grade if the child is a poor reader at the end of first grade.
- One in six children who are not reading proficiently in the third grade do not graduate from high school on time, a rate four times greater than that for proficient readers.
- Sixty-eight percent of America's fourth graders read at a level below proficiency, and 82% of those children are from low-income families.

Literacy Essentials

As you can see, the data related to the importance of literacy and how low-literacy levels continue to "hamstring" our students in school and thereafter are striking. Sound instructional leadership requires an acknowledgment that any education improvement efforts not focused on literacy will be severely limited in their impact. This acknowledgment is critical because the only guaranteed way to improve learning and true college and career readiness comes by way of literacy. High school leaders must accept that literacy is about more than the visual that too often pops into minds, which tends to be small children reading aloud or being read to. Rather, as Vicki Phillips and Carina Wong put it, "Think of literacy as the spine; it holds everything together. The branches of learning connect to it, meaning that all content teachers have a responsibility to teach literacy" (Schmoker, 2011).

We must recognize that in order to successfully define literacy and leverage it to improve learning, we must note that it is the composition of purposeful reading, annotation/note-taking, writing, and discussion that are the basis of literacy. These four components must be understood and leveraged so that they drive your instructional planning and delivery. This notion is further supported by the Knowledge and Skills necessary for University Success (KSUS). The KSUS is based on the research and collaboration of the best and most prominent colleges and

Simple. Practical. Effective.

universities in the nation. The KSUS is aligned with Common Core's College and Career Readiness (CCR) standards. The following is a brief description of each of these literacy components and how their role is vital to learning and developing a deep understanding of any content's material. The effective instructional leaders embrace the nuances of these components and seek to make them the bedrock of the school's plan for achieving its purpose and goals.

***Reading Comprehension** - "Reading is Fundamental," and lack of strong literacy skills is debilitating not only to academic success but also to productive citizenship. Thus, all teachers should know, understand, and consistently implement reading strategies. The human mind, for the most part, can only acquire and integrate new knowledge through reading, discussion, and experience. Through literature and comprehension, you can ensure that students can make sense of the world and the workforce we are preparing them to enter. Consequently, reading comprehension must permeate all content area instruction; this will ensure that students have the background knowledge across content areas to succeed at the university level and in their chosen careers. Simply put, if you cannot comprehend, you cannot be successful. Remember, like the "Matthew Effect," knowledge builds on knowledge, and the more you know, the more you can learn.

***Annotation/Note-taking** - Note-taking is a critical component of learning. Students should be taught and expected to take detailed notes, and they should be held accountable for having and studying these notes. Note-taking helps to ensure that students are engaged in the learning process and have written evidence of what was taught, learned, and discussed in class. Note-taking also helps students organize their thoughts in a systematic way that makes sense to them. As a result, these notes become more meaningful to students and better ensure that they understand the content. Cornell Notes and various other note-taking templates and graphic organizers can be used to help students learn this crucial skill. As students mature, they should develop their own effective methods for taking notes. Annotating and note-taking should be evident in daily instruction across all content areas.

***Writing and Editing** - Some would argue that effective writing skills are amongst the most important indicators of 21stcentury workforce success. Further, the writing and revision processes require the highest levels of cognitive demand (analysis, synthesis, and evaluation), and writing helps us to communicate our thoughts with clarity and precision. New data show that the information age now requires us to write more than ever before. Yet, there has been a precipitous decline in the amount of writing required in K-12 schools. Students need to write often. All written assignments should be graded for grammar. Proper sentence structure and correct grammar usage are prerequisites for effective writing. Good writing improves reading comprehension and vice versa, and writing improves students' critical thinking; there is a great deal of critical thought involved in writing for various purposes and audiences. There is no way every teacher can be a grammar expert, but schools or departments within schools can focus on three grammar/syntax issues that tend to be evident at every level of education. These tend to be: (a) subject-verb agreement, (b) matching of pronouns and their antecedents, and (c) consistent and proper use of tenses. Certainly, there is an array of other grammar and language conventions to choose from. The key is to be consistent in the grading and correcting of the identified areas. College courses are rigorous in their writing requirements, as are many employers, so schools must begin teaching students effective writing. By the time students exit high school, they should be able to construct 3-5 page argumentative and expository papers that are coherent and grammatically sound. Outline development along with consistent drafting and revising of written assignments should be expected; revising is a key component to acquiring effective writing skills.

*Discussion - Discussion, which includes speaking and listening, will aid students in developing sound thought processes and a clear rationale for their thinking. It also provides a means for students' thoughts to be explored and challenged. Couched in the academic discussion are opportunities for students to learn how to collaborate and appropriately challenge one another for the sake of intellectual growth. Well managed discussion and debates afford students opportunities to learn the democratic process through the exchange of ideas, and this skill is important to students' development as citizens and as learners. These discussions can take on the form of pair sharing, small group/recitation style discussions, presentations, Socratic discussions, and debates. Further, many of today's information age jobs require successful collaboration in the spirit of problem-solving. Speaking and listening are the cornerstones of effective collaboration and, in many cases, for success in the workforce.

In reviewing those instructional focus areas, one might be apt to challenge the rather simplistic nature of those focuses. After all, there is nothing novel about reading, annotating, discussing, and writing. Nonetheless, these focuses are the foundation upon which all learning is predicated. Simply put, if students are not engaged in reading, annotating, discussing, and writing, they are not learning. Now, as with all things, the extent to which these focus areas bring about the desired levels of improvement is a function of how clearly they are understood, applied to specific content areas, and implemented in an effective manner. The role of the instructional leader is to communicate the importance of these literacy focus areas, ensure staff have a set of techniques that support each focus, and guarantee that these focuses are the drivers of instructional observations, discussions, and feedback. In essence, these focus areas offer a duality in the sense that it is their simplicity that underwrites, when implemented effectively, students' abilities to think critically about a topic or subject area. I would surmise that most people reading this book are enrolled in or have completed masters or doctoral level coursework. Thus, you should understand that the core of your learning and ability to think critically has been borne out of your ability and time spent reading, annotating, discussing, and writing about your professional craft or personal experiences and interests.

Figure 3 is a visual of these focus areas and how they move learners from "learning to learn" to "learning to think" while setting the foundation for critical thinking.

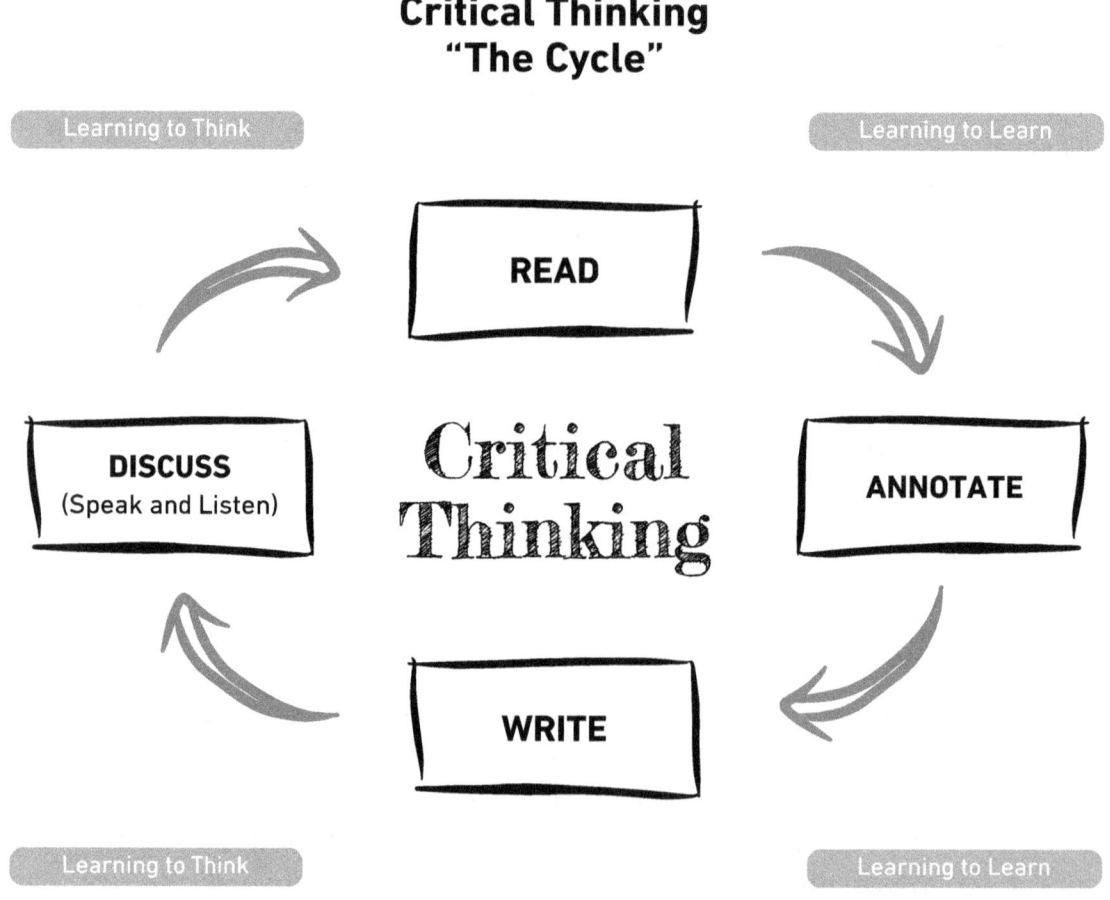

Figure 3: **The Critical Thinking Cycle**

Again, the impactful nature of focusing on these essential elements of literacy applied across content areas cannot be overstated. It is a well-established fact that one of the strongest and most reliable predictors of student achievement is literacy, and, as data consistently demonstrate, students who struggle in reading have lower graduation rates, pass state assessments at lower levels, are suspended at higher rates, etc. when compared to their grade-level peers who read at or above grade level. Henceforth, a focus on literacy is not just an educational priority; it is a moral imperative, and it has to be the focal point of any plan for improvement. Leaders who choose not to imbue a profound focus on literacy as their plan have in a proverbial sense "lost the game before it had even started."

Lesson Planning for Literacy-Based Instruction

After embracing the vital nature of literacy as the foundation on which the plan should be built, the effective instructional leader needs to turn one's attention to creating the conditions by which literacy can become prevalent in daily teaching and learning. There is an axiom that states "failing to prepare is preparing for failure." Take this axiom and substitute the word plan for prepare and the statement still holds true. Any noteworthy accomplishment is derived from focused planning that entails a series of well-thought out ideas and coordinated actions. Whether it is a chess player placing an opponent into a "check position," NASA launching a shuttle into the far reaches of outer space, a corporation seeking to increase its market capitalization, or a master teacher orchestrating an effectual lesson, the fact remains that thoughtful planning is at the root of all of these tasks and accomplishments. The plan, as noted, must be simple and straightforward enough to be understood and enacted effectively.

Far too often, educators devise planning processes that are too unfocused and complex. In doing so, their desired outcome is nearly unattainable from the outset because the plan is not connected to a clear purpose with intentional processes. Madeline Hunter understood this notion when she developed her lesson planning model decades ago. Her planning model was founded on a straightforward approach to planning lessons tightly aligned with the intended learning outcomes. Ms. Hunter's lesson plan components included a clear objective, anticipatory set, modeling, guided practice, independent practice, and closure. Each component of the lesson is essential, and for those who have observed the best lessons they know, firsthand, that these lessons flow like an exceptionally well-written poem or movie script (Hunter, 2004).

However, over the years and decades, educators seem to have drifted from these essential lesson planning components in favor of what is believed to be "21st century approaches" that have done nothing more than "muddy the waters" for teachers. Critics of well-defined, structured approaches like that of Madeline Hunter's will likely argue that it is not well suited for exploratory learning or the teaching of higher-order thinking skills, but they will cite little to no credible evidence backing that notion. Often, these "novel approaches" to lesson planning are derived from a yearning for change for change's sake and not focused on effectiveness. Let me be clear, change for the sake of change is not synonymous with improvement. As the saying goes, "If it ain't broke, then don't fix it." While the students we interface with and the technology we use continue to change, the fundamentals of creating a sound lesson plan have not; sound lesson planning that incorporates the essential components of literacy ensure higher levels of learning and increased capacity for critical thinking. In this regard, we must resist the urge to shift to "flashier" approaches and instead get back to the basics of purposeful lesson planning.

As leaders devise their approach to planning, they must be insistent that all of the essential elements of Madeline Hunter's plan are included. This is not to say that the language cannot be modified, nor does it mean that the lesson cannot contain more than her essential components. Nevertheless, at the base of your planning must be those elements that are tried and true and have been proven to elevate student learning. In this vein, when I was a principal, my leadership team and I formulated what we called, interchangeably, the 6M or M&Ms planning model. To certify that the approach was sound and that each component was linked to one another, we crafted a rationale for each of the components. Each component was also connected to Charlotte Danielson's Framework for Teaching (FFT) and demanded the incorporation of literacy skills into and throughout the lesson. The following is a brief description of each component of the 6M planning model:

Measurable Objective - *(1C: Setting Instructional Outcomes)*

A clear and measurable objective, aligned to the curriculum, serves as the foundation for planning a sound lesson. The objective should be concise (typically less than 15 words), and it should, referencing language from Bloom's Taxonomy, clearly articulate what students will "know and be able to do" by the end of the lesson. In conjunction with objectives, agendas are a great way to communicate what steps the class will take to achieve mastery of the objective. Agendas can help with lesson pacing and provide students a clear understanding of what the lesson will entail.

Motivational Activity - *(1B: Demonstrating Knowledge of Students)*

The motivational activity serves as the "hook" that brings the objective to life and engages the learner. This lesson segment is critical to setting the purpose for learning and engaging students. Furthermore, the motivational activity should help students understand the "purpose" of the day's lesson and aid them in understanding how the lesson applies to their lives and or the real world; this is the essence of making learning relevant. Motivational activities are a great instructional area for the infusion of technology and the use of compelling, real-world questions, issues, and scenarios. A great motivational activity is akin to a great movie trailer that piques your interest, leaving you wanting to see and learn more.

Modeling - *(1A: Demonstrating Knowledge of Content/Pedagogy)*

Modeling affords the teacher an opportunity to explicitly "show and/or tell" (visual and audio) students the processes needed for solving problems and answering questions. The step by step modeling of the teacher's thoughts helps students develop the rationale and habits of mind needed to ensure learning. Explicit modeling is the first component of the "I, We, You" modeling process.

However, it is not always developmentally appropriate to employ such an explicit and didactic approach to modeling. The modeling process can also be inquiry-driven and, therefore, address higher-order thinking skills. In these instances, the teacher can pose a question or problem and then step back as students attempt to use their requisite knowledge to solve the problem. As students report out, the teacher serves as a facilitator and validates their answer or guides them to the correct answer. This is known as the "You, We, You" modeling process. This approach is often cited as a centerpiece of instruction in those eastern Asian countries that often perform at or near the top on international assessments like The Programme for International Student Assessment (PISA).

Meaningful Steps - *(1E: Designing Coherent Instruction; 1D: Demonstrating Knowledge of Resources)*

Meaningful "lesson steps" are various lesson activities that are all tightly aligned to moving students toward an understanding of the objective. For each of the chosen lesson steps, the teacher should be able to answer HOW (knowledge of content) the lesson step will move students toward the intended learning and WHY he or she chose this particular lesson activity for this particular group of students (knowledge of students). Infused in these lesson steps should be multiple opportunities to read, annotate, write, and discuss. Constant checks for understanding in the form of formative assessments must also be embedded in each of the lesson steps.

Make Sure - *(1F: Designing Student Assessments)*

Making sure is simply a way to check for mastery of the objective. This is often referred to as an assessment, and it can be the lesson's independent practice, a summative assessment, or an "exit ticket." The lesson plan should include well-thought out formative and summative assessments. This information should provide the teacher with a clear understanding of students' levels of understanding of the day's lesson. It is imperative that the teacher use the information gleaned from the assessments to determine the extent to which students achieved the lesson's learning target. Equipped with this information, the teacher will better understand students in need of additional or differentiated support and ensure these areas are revisited in subsequent lessons.

Make Connections - *(1A: Demonstrating Knowledge of Content/ Pedagogy: 1C: Setting Instructional Outcomes)*

Making connections provides closure to the lesson. As a wrap-up to the day's lesson, the teacher should take a few moments to ensure that students understand how the day's lesson connects with the next step, future learning, and or how the day's lesson will be of value to them in a real-world context. The importance of closure cannot be overstated. Closure provides opportunities for students to reflect on their learning and to grasp the relevance between what they learned and how it will impact their learning from that point forward.

Figure 4 is a sample lesson plan format illustrating the application of these key lesson planning components as well as the thought processes and guiding questions needed to formulate a coherent plan for teaching and learning.

Figure 4: ***6M Planning Model Template***

ABC High School
6M Planning Model

Teacher Name:_____   Subject:_____

Day/Date		
Unit		
Indicator		
Measurable Objective		
SCOPE AND SEQUENCE OF THE LESSON		**TIME**
Review of Previous Lesson (Drill)		
Motivational Activity Guiding Question: 1. What is the relevance of this activity? Why do you believe it will "hook" the students?		
Modeling Guiding Questions: 1. Why did you use this modeling approach? 2. Do the students have the requisite knowledge for an exploratory approach?		

Meaningful Steps Guiding Questions: Note: For each "lesson step," please be able to answer: 1. "How" it supports mastering the objective? 2. "Why" you chose this particular strategy/method for this group of students? 3. "What" you will do if students don't "get it"? 4. "How" does this step account for our literacy focus areas?		
Make Sure (Summary/Assessment) Guiding Questions: 1. Does your summative assessment align with your objective based on Bloom's Taxonomy? 2. How will you use this assessment information?		
Make Connections Guiding Question: 1. How will you connect the day's learning to next steps, future learning, and do so in a meaningful way?		
Homework		

Supporting Effective Lesson Planning with Driving Questions

The following is a resource containing "driving questions" that assist teachers in planning lessons that are intentional in their alignment to standards and relevant to student interests and needs. These questions can also serve as pre-conference discussion questions in the clinical observation model.

Figure 5: **Pre-conference Driving Questions**

Pre-conference Questions

Course   : _____

Lesson Unit   : _____

Lesson Objective : _____

Motivational Activity:

Please briefly explain your motivational activity, its connection to the lesson objective, and how it helps students understand and reinforces the value of the day's lesson.

Modeling:

Is modeling necessary? If so, will your approach be gradual release or exploratory/inquiry based in nature? Why did you choose this modeling approach?

Lesson Steps:

For <u>each</u> of your lesson steps (activities), please explain:

1. How does it support helping students to understand and master the objective?
2. Why did you choose this strategy for this group/class of students?

3. What challenges or issues do you anticipate as students complete this lesson step /activity? How have you planned to address these issues or challenges as they arise?
4. How will you ensure that literacy is embedded in each of lesson steps?

Make Sure:

How will you gauge/measure students' understanding throughout and at the end of the lesson?

Make Connections:

How will you close this lesson by making connections back to the objective and or to future learning?

As evident, these questions are aligned to the 6M lesson planning model shown as Figure 4. They ensure there is a clearly defined structure and process for lesson planning standards and expectations. The clarity provided by these questions can aid teachers in "fleshing out" their lesson ideas and organizing the lesson in a coherent manner that best positions their students to grasp the material. While many of the best teachers think through these questions naturally and intuitively, others do not and will benefit from this kind of guidance. As an effective instructional leader, one of your biggest tasks is to create processes that ensure all teachers can be successful.

CHAPTER 5

Supporting Literacy-Focused Instruction

Meaningful Appraisal - What Gets Monitored Gets Done

Most school leaders are bound to a prescribed process and "tool" when conducting formal observations. This is likely a process and tool that has been agreed upon and approved by system officials and bargaining unit representatives. Unfortunately, given the bureaucratic manner in which these agreements are reached, there is a chance the process and tool used to gauge teachers' effectiveness are based on, at least in part, variables that have more to do with "standardization and fairness" than they do with teachers' improvement. My point here is not intended to demean teachers or the negotiation process, but rather my point is to encourage school leaders to recognize that building teachers' capacity, which is the ultimate driver of school improvement, requires meaningful appraisal. Truly building teachers' capacities requires much more than what can be achieved in limited, formal observations that may or may not be aligned to your school's focuses or priorities.

Fortunately, as a school leader, you likely have much in the way of freedom with regards to your informal observation processes and tools. While the formal observation is certainly a high-stakes estimation connected to a teacher's overall evaluation, the informal observation process can be leveraged as an endeavor centered on teachers' improvement. Informal observations are best when understood and viewed as a formative assessment of teaching used to gauge the extent to which the teacher is successfully meeting students' learning needs. Further, informal observations can be crafted to help school leaders glean insight into planning and pedagogical trends, issues, and successes. To draw on a sports analogy, the informal observation is an "inner-squad" scrimmage that provides the coach and players the information needed to refine their "game plan and its execution." The informal observation can be differentiated by department, course, or teacher, and can be designed so it is congruent with a school's instructional focus areas and planning model. With all that said, school leaders would be wise to create an informal observation tool that clearly aligns with and incorporates their focus areas and planning model. If not, then the informal observation tool will likely be perceived as tangential and will not support teachers in planning and implementing robust lessons.

Knowing the importance of connecting teacher feedback with our instructional priorities, along with my leadership team, I led the development of an informal observation tool and process that ensured regular, ongoing teacher feedback banked against those areas we knew to be most essential to improving student learning. A few things were kept in mind during the development of the said tool. First, as discussed, the tool had to be aligned with our determined instructional focuses. Second, it had to offer specific narrative feedback that was "chunked and concise," so teachers could easily understand and act on this feedback. We were adamant that a move toward checklist style informal observations, while efficient, would not suffice in supporting improvement. After all, processes for improving teaching should not be reduced to checklists and checkboxes. What teachers do is far too intricate to be reduced to such a futile approach to providing feedback. Third, our leadership team had to commit to developing a process for completing these informal observations, discussing them, and determining ideas that would assist leadership team members (administrators and department chairpersons) in acting on this information in the name of improvement. Figure 6 is a sample copy of our tool.

Figure 6: *Informal Visit Feedback Form*

ABC High School Informal Visit Feedback

Observer : _____   Teacher   : _____

Subject   : _____   Date/Time : _____

6M Planning Model	Feedback
— Measurable Objective • Use of Bloom's Taxonomy • What and How • Use of Agenda **— Motivational Activity** • Hook that brings obj. to life/sets purpose • Real Word Connection/Activates prior knowledge • Good place to infuse technology **— Modeling** • Gradual (I, We, You) • Exploration/Inquiry (You, We, You) • Frequent Checks for Understanding **— Meaningful Steps** • Guided by How and Why • Offers Differentiation • Frequent Checks for Understanding • Reading • Annotation • Writing (Written Communication) • Critical Thinking/Problem Solving • Discussion **— Make Sure!** • Summative check for understanding • Could be the independent practice or Exit Slip • "Data" to help drive next step planning **— Make Connections (Closure)** • Connections back to Motivational Activity • Connections to next step learning	• *Was there evidence of Reading? Yes/ No* _____ _____ _____ • *Was there evidence of Annotating/Note-taking? Yes/ No* _____ _____ _____ • *Was there evidence of Writing? Yes/ No* _____ _____ _____ • *Was there evidence of Discussion? Yes/ No* _____ _____ _____ • *Was there evidence of Effective Management? Yes/ No* _____ _____ _____

Once you have successfully developed an informal observation tool, you must then create a structured plan for the use of this tool. This structured plan must ensure that informal observations are conducted regularly and used to leverage pedagogical improvement. Comprehensive high school principals are fortunate in that they are often supported by a leadership team that includes department chairpersons as well as assistant principals. The department chairpersons serve as your "content experts" and, thus, are able to assess the extent to which the content is aligned to the appropriate standards and if the content is being conveyed to the students accurately. The administrators, the principal and assistant principals, serve as your "pedagogical generalists" who can hone in on the extent to which sound teaching practices are evident. These practices include aspects of teaching such as the appropriateness of the lesson plan, lesson pacing and transitions, student engagement, and the extent to which the school's instructional focuses are incorporated in the lesson. In many instances, a cluster of departments is assigned to each assistant principal who can work closely with the respective chairpersons to support the plan to provide informal, growth-centered feedback to teachers.

A structured plan for leveraging informal observations would include the following:

1. Each department determines the frequency of informal observations to be conducted for each staff member. In my experience, this should be differentiated with more visits to novice teachers and those who have struggled to meet with success. The number should be based on a per month factor.

2. Once you have determined these frequencies, the department chairperson and administrator (principal or assistant principal) should work collaboratively to create a schedule to conduct these informal observations.

3. Observations should be conducted in accordance with this schedule, and immediate feedback should be provided to the teachers.

4. Copies of each informal observation conducted in a particular month should be archived and maintained by the leadership team.

5. Each month, the department chairperson and administrator should meet to review the informal observation reports in aggregate to determine department needs moving forward. These findings can help determine subsequent department meeting focuses. Further, this information will illustrate those who are excelling versus those who are struggling and could lead to peer observation and coaching opportunities. This monthly debriefing also builds school leaders' instructional leadership capacity.

Tying it All Together with your Professional Development Plan

As discussed in Chapter 2, one of the key components of the core four is "people." It is certainly plausible to believe that most leaders comprehend the importance of recruiting the "right people." However, it seems to be less likely that these same leaders understand the crucial role they, themselves, need to play in investing in people. Investing in and "growing" your people will not only set the conditions for improvement, but it will also increase people's engagement as well as their commitment. It will guard against burnout and attrition rates. Consider the following logic chain: We know that supporting and investing in people increases staff stability. This stability has a direct impact on improvement efforts. Improvement efforts ensure that the students are in receipt of a quality education and, thus, are better prepared for the rigors of college and the workforce. Clearly, investing in your people and their capacity pays dividends. Therefore, careful attention must be paid to your staff development plan. It must be simple enough to execute successfully while also providing a structure that ensures teachers have ample opportunities to pursue excellence in their instruction.

The Age-Long Debate: A Need for a Blended Approach

Those of us familiar with the generation-long debate regarding literacy instruction know that this discourse pitted those who championed a "whole language" approach to reading versus those who espoused "phonics-based instruction." After years of fervent banter, research on reading instruction revealed that neither whole language nor phonics-based instruction in isolation maximized literacy learning. Rather, it is a careful combination and the balancing of the two approaches that best ensures students are equipped with the reading levels that set them on the path to succeed in school and in life.

A similar debate permeates conversations related to staff development. In the case of staff development, there seems to be subtle, yet divergent thinking about the importance and impact of staff development that is content-focused juxtaposed with staff development that is pedagogy-focused. Typically, elementary and middle schools are organized by grade level teams that place pedagogy and student well-being at the core of staff development and collaborative meetings. Meanwhile, high schools are most often organized by content area departments. By design, high schools are better positioned to emphasize teacher collaboration and improvement that is content-specific in nature. Both approaches are essential to enrich teacher and student learning. Analogous to the reading example, it is important that school leaders strike a balance between content-focused and pedagogy-focused learning when framing their staff development plan. Further, and just as importantly, the staff development plan must successfully braid depth of content knowledge, breadth of pedagogy, and your instructional focus areas in a manner that is seamless. A best practice for achieving this end is to utilize professional learning communities and vertical teaming meetings.

Professional Learning Teams

The term "professional learning team" is a play on words. Most, if not all, educational leaders are at least somewhat familiar with professional learning communities or PLC. As a principal, I was always looking for ways to drive home the importance of collaboration and singularity of purpose. A team, by its very nature, exemplifies collaboration, connectedness, and commitment to a selfless purpose. Thus, I moved to modify the word "communities" in favor of the word "team." At the high school level, leaders can organize their PLTs using several methods. However, knowing that the customary structure of high schools is one that favors content area collaboration, I viewed PLTs as a means of focusing on cross-curricular, pedagogy-focused dialogue. That is, a PLT can be arranged in a way that allows teachers from varying departments to discuss and share the most effective strategies and techniques for a multitude of instructional focuses. However, as noted, there is no other set of instructional focuses that proximate literacy in terms of their impact on learning across all content areas. Accordingly, as an instructional leader, one would be well-advised in organizing PLTs around a particular aspect of literacy, the most meaningful of which are reading and writing.

For those who are familiar with the work that came out of the famed "Brockton High School," you will recollect that their focus on school-wide writing initiatives was said to be the primary contributing factor in their improvement efforts. This was done by way of creating clear expectations for the writing process and then engaging in school-wide dialogue and collaboration about the process. To this day, the work done at Brockton stands as a model for large scale meaningful improvement at the high school level. In my experience as an educator and as a student myself, I can make a compelling case for why writing is the ideal learning process on which a PLT can stand. Writing is certainly among the most rigorous academic exercises as it requires one to hold a depth of understanding regarding the content being referenced, an expansive content-related vocabulary, patience and concentration, and a command of language structures and conventions. As you move into and throughout college, writing becomes increasingly commonplace. Some of us can still recall having our first college essay returned drenched in red ink to reinforce how ill-prepared we were as writers despite our "glowing" grade point averages in high school. I make all these points to support the notion that there is great value in a school-wide approach to improved writing for students.

Once you determine your PLT literacy focus, you are then ready to structure your PLT in a purposeful manner. Assuming your chosen focus is writing, you then work with your leadership team to determine the type (or types) of prose you will center your meetings on. Argumentative writing is a great place to start; this style of writing requires researching a topic so claims and counterclaims can be supported. It also requires one to construct a persuasive thesis as well as convincing concluding points. Thus, argumentative writing can easily be structured into the well-known "five-paragraph essay," which can be assigned across contents and serve as a means to assess student writing. Next, you can work to determine the most critical elements of that prose. These elements then serve as the foundation for the development of a school-wide rubric. This rubric, in turn, becomes the basis for the various aspects of writing, through which teachers can infuse into their lessons and ultimately reflect on during their PLT meetings. During such meetings, staff will share writing activities they have implemented, how those activities align to the rubric's focuses, share how they are assessing students' writing abilities, and receive feedback from their peers on how they can enhance their efforts to improve student writing. This continuous loop of planning and implementing strategies, sharing those strategies, and then refining those efforts by way of peer feedback and collaboration runs parallel to the well-known "plan, do, study, act" systemic improvement model. Who you place in a PLT is less important than having clear structures and expectations for the process.

Vertical Teaming

Alongside PLCs or PLTs should be a process that allows staff to collaborate directly with their content area colleagues. At the secondary level, the department meeting should be arranged in a manner that lends meeting time to vertical teaming as well as same-course collaboration. In just about all high schools, these meetings are present in the staff development plan. However, too often, the content and flow of these meetings account for neither the important nature of deepening content knowledge nor the discussion of the very best ways of conveying that knowledge in support of student learning. In my experience of working alongside principals and supervising them, in many instances, department meetings are glorified sit-and-get-information, update/sharing sessions with little to no emphasis placed on the learning of standards and the delivery of instruction. Please note these updates should be communicated in a matter of minutes or through a different medium altogether. Staff development time tends to be a scarce resource in many schools, so when you pull a group of educators together for a meeting, the expectation must be to make them better instructors.

As mentioned in the section on informal observations, these meetings should use data gleaned from classroom observations to establish opportunities for vertical teaming; that is, ensuring that teachers of sequential courses have time to collaborate, so each can better understand what students are expected to learn in courses prior to and after each course in the sequence. As an example, your Algebra I teacher should have time to dialogue with your Geometry or Algebra II teacher so he or she better understands those standards that are essential to success in the following course or courses. While this process is invaluable in establishing coherence between courses, it is most critical when working to establish and grow enrollment in your most rigorous course levels. These typically include Honors, Gifted and Talented (G&T), Advanced Placement (AP), or International Baccalaureate (IB) level courses. Simply put, the vertical teaming process allows you to determine and share information relating to the academic profile of students who succeed in higher-level courses, and it allows the sharing of the instructional expectations in these courses. For instance, if you establish that students who succeed in AP United States History read and comprehend for extended periods of time, let's say 45 minutes, and are astute at using the information illuminated from the text to accurately respond to document-based questions by citing evidence, then this skill set and expectation must be shared with teachers who teach courses prior to AP United States History.

Armed with this knowledge, these teachers are better positioned to assign work that scaffolds accordingly and lays the foundation for students to be successful in the most rigorous of courses. You can apply this example across all contents, whether it be mathematics, science, English, or career and technology completers. Understanding what it takes to be successful in high-level courses and backward mapping strategies for moving all students toward that end is a means of equity. For those former athletes and coaches, vertical teaming ensures the freshmen team is prepping student-athletes for junior varsity, which is, in turn, preparing student-athletes for success at the varsity level. In the context of succession planning in hierarchical organizations, each person is responsible for teaching the people "behind them" their job while also learning the job of the "person in front of them." Vertical teaming applies this concept to planning, instruction, and assessment.

While not technically "vertical" in nature, same course collaboration, or horizontal collaboration, is also essential to improving instructional practice. In large high schools, there are usually cohorts of teachers who teach the same courses and course levels. This is an asset that can also be leveraged during department meetings. Teachers of the same courses can work together to strengthen their understanding of the content, and they can work together in mapping out curriculum. These teachers can also collaborate on the development of assessments aligned to course standards and the planning of lessons that best ensure students can master the material. Finally, these teachers are able to share course-related student data and work to establish reteaching and intervention plans to support students who were unable to demonstrate proficiency on course work and assessments. While some schools have common planning time for some same course teachers, others do not as it does not always lend itself to scheduling efficiency. Whether the meetings take place during common planning or during department meetings, the key is to ensure that there are structured protocols for focusing these meetings on those collaborative discussion topics referenced in my prior sentences. If not, these meetings divert attention toward superficial matters and complaining, none of which have any impact on improving teaching and learning.

Department meetings should also be inclusive of time for your teachers to discuss practices for effectively conveying content to students, especially with regards to those topics and concepts students often struggle to grasp. Staff who have demonstrated success as observed in informal and formal observations should be highlighted and encouraged to share those teaching practices that have served their students well. There are innumerable ways to organize these meetings, but you have to be able to do so in a manner that supports teacher growth. By focusing department meetings on content-specific knowledge and pedagogy, you are setting the foundation for teacher learning and improved student achievement.

Structuring Your Plan

As discussed, a great way to leverage school-wide improvement in literacy while also sharpening teachers' content-specific capabilities, is to create a staff development structure that sets the conditions for both. As a high school principal, my staff and I were able to achieve this balance by organizing our professional development into PLTs and department meetings. Now, I fully understand that there might be a need for more "ad hoc" staff development, but, by and large, the blended model discussed in this section, when done with genuine effort and efficacy, can be impactful and maximize teacher learning while supporting student and school needs. As mentioned, there is a need for flexibility in staff development, and you can create this flexibility in how you organize your PLTs and department meetings. Further, principals should look to utilize differentiated job-embedded staff development, which can take the form of peer observations, learning walks, and collaborative planning meetings, to list a few. However, PLTs and vertical teaming should form the foundation of your staff development plan. Below is Figure 7, which illustrates a simple, practical, and effective means for organizing a staff development plan.

Figure 7: **Staff Development Action Plan Template**

ABC High School – Staff Development Action Plan

Developing & Refining Quality Core Instruction through the Effective Implementation of our Instructional Focus Areas - Purposeful Reading, Writing, Discussion, and Annotating

Goal 1: Improve Teacher Effectiveness via collaboration	Action/Strategy	Person(s) Responsible	Date
Indicator 1.1	**Presentation**: *Connecting the ABC Planning and Instructional Focus Framework to improved achievement and to Danielson*	Principal	Aug
Indicator 1.2	**Presentation:** School-wide Student Learning Outcomes (SLOs) - Argumentative Writing	APs	Aug/ Jan

Indicator 1.3	Bi-weekly Department Meetings focused on Vertical Teaming in the areas of: (a) grading, (b) planning and designing of assessments, (c) literacy expectations, (d) course leveling and expectations, (d) homework expectations, etc.	Chairs/ All	Bi-weekly
Indicator 1.4	Bi-monthly PLTs for "cross-curricular" sharing of effective techniques for writing across content areas *see attached schedule/PLT meeting outline*	Chairs/ All	Nov/ Monthly
Goal 2: Improve Teacher effectiveness via the appraisal process	**Action/Strategy**	**Person(s) Responsible**	**Date**
Indicator 2.1	Formal observation process by system guidelines	Admin/ Chairs	Quarterly
Indicator 2.2	Informal observations and the differentiated improvement model (Instructional Rounds, Learning Walks, Peer Observation, Action Research, etc.) **Framework for Teaching-Domain 4*	Chairs/ Teachers	Monthly
Indicator 2.3	Individual Classroom Management/Planning Sessions for Year 1 Teachers	Teacher Leader(s)	Quarterly

SUMMARY

Having fundamentally sound and well-thought out structures and processes are imperative to success as an instructional leader. Further, these structures and processes must align in a manner that ensures they are all supporting the same outcome. The effective instructional leader can clearly articulate the alignment of such structures and how those structures support the school's priorities and improvement endeavors. In doing so, the leader can crystalize her or his instructional leadership with a demonstrable "Plan" that guides the work that the "People" have been asked to carry out. If you want to gauge the extent to which a school leader is truly engaged in the work of enhancing teaching and boosting student learning, ask him or her a few simple questions, including:

1. What are the school's foremost instructional focuses?
2. What was the rationale for identifying these focuses?
3. What are the essential elements and expectations for lesson planning?
4. How does the school's professional development plan support teacher growth in your instructional focus areas while also building their content knowledge?
5. How will you monitor and measure the success of these efforts?

While the information discussed in this chapter and the subsequent answers to these questions might come across as basic, they are important pillars to your success as a school leader. Remember, effectiveness is preceded by simplicity and practicality. The best principals whom I have worked alongside or supervised can answer these questions with certainty, clarity, and with little hesitation. Further, these principals are able to provide well-detailed plans and documents framing the work that is being done as it relates to the five questions referenced above. If you want to be an effective instructional leader, then you should start first by creating mechanisms that address what was discussed in this chapter. In doing so, you will have established the foundation for your efforts to operationalize instructional leadership by turning ideas into action. The next step is enacting strategic action plans designed to further support your efforts to ensure students graduate high school on time and well-prepared for college and the workforce. The action plans discussed and presented in succeeding chapters focus on aiding school leaders with this next step.

PART III
ACTION PLANNING

CHAPTER 6

Strategic Planning for College and Career Readiness

Planning for Readiness

Recall that earlier there was a discussion of the shift from college and career eligible to college and career ready. Here, in this part of the book, we return to those metrics that serve as markers for moving students from eligible to ready. Before moving into the strategy and planning that goes into achieving progress toward these metrics, it was essential that the foundational components of instructional leadership were established. Now it is time to turn attention to the strategic planning process. As you will see, these action plans and strategies are heavily contingent upon and tethered to the foremost instructional leadership priority, which is establishing literacy as the cornerstone of your efforts. By doing so, you are likely to ensure students are ready for the post-secondary and work-related challenges that await them upon their departure from high school. In these plans, particularly in the "effective middle to high school transition plan (ACE)" and the "SAT and AP action plans," you will see the embedding of a deliberate focus on literacy. Again, these plans, just like all the resources shared in this book, are not necessarily meant to be a "prescribed or canned" model. Rather, they are examples of how the right focuses combined with the well-thought out processes can

Simple. Practical. Effective.

be harnessed into plans and strategies that fuel improvement. Figure 2 is again shown below as a reminder of the visual concept of how these three markers can be posts that guide your efforts.

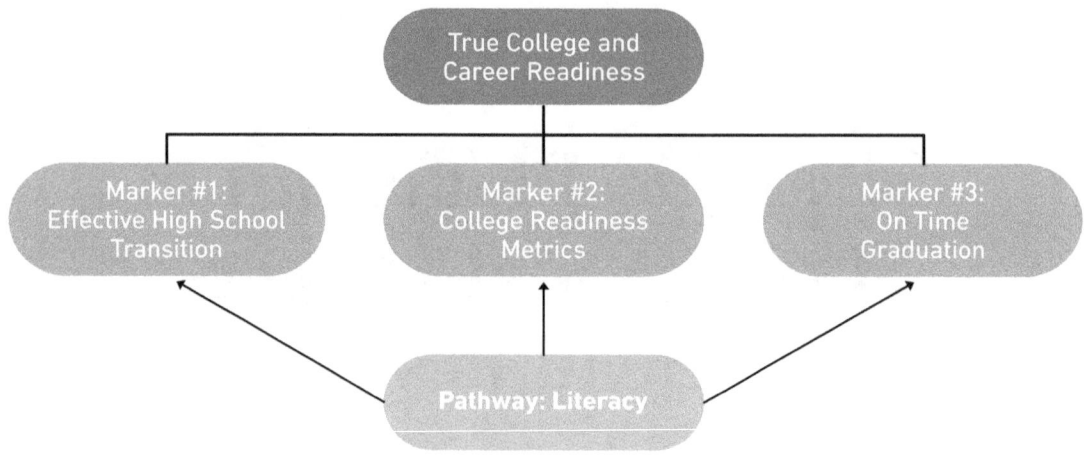

Figure 2: **A Pathway to College and Career Readiness**

The following is a description and discussion of the strategies that undergird these plans. Effective transitions are discussed first, followed by SAT and AP action planning. Subsequent to these plans, there is a discussion on how to ensure students persist to graduation, especially during their senior year. Please note that the order of these plans is, indeed, intentional and sequential. Graduating high school college and workforce ready is unlikely to happen in the absence of a transition plan that equips 9th grade students with the skills and habits of mind to be serious learners and effective consumers of knowledge. These skills and habits, in turn, support students' preparedness for high-level courses, and in this case AP courses, as well as achieving desirable scores on the SAT.

CHAPTER 7

Effective Middle to High School Transition

Action Plan - The Power of ACE

It is generally accepted that each step in the K-12 continuum has a substantial influence on students' college and workforce readiness. However, there's strong evidence suggesting the middle school to high school transition is among the most important factors in determining students' success in high school, preparedness for college, and in achieving success in their chosen careers. Further, transition issues transcend school types and impact student success in urban, suburban, and rural schools. Yet, despite this nearly conclusive understanding of the importance of this transition, a limited number of meaningful reform efforts have been implemented to address successful middle to high school transitions.

Fully cognizant of the importance of this transition, my school leadership team crafted a transition plan anchored by three components, with each component viewed as an essential aspect of successfully transitioning students into high school and placing students on a trajectory to truly being college and career ready. The acronym ACE, which stands for academics, character, and extension, served as the anchor upon which school leadership framed the program. Each of the program's anchors was supported by a series of goals and indicators designed to guide the program's implementation.

Simple. Practical. Effective.

ACE Program Structure:

To ensure the sound implementation of the program, school leadership designed several essential organizational structures. A brief outline and description of the program structures are presented below.

First, a "teaming model" was used to support teacher collaboration within and across content areas. The teaming model offers opportunities for students to build stronger relationships among their peers and can improve school and parent communication. Students were hand scheduled onto each team using a "systematic heterogeneous" placement method based on academic abilities determined by eighth-grade assessments. The teams were again balanced to ensure equality in terms of race, gender, and special needs composition. The teaming model was further predicated on multiple cross-curricular teams, each of which was comprised of an English, math, science, and social studies teacher working together to support approximately 125 students. This structure enables each team of teachers to better understand students' needs, have closer connections to students, and helps with employing a more holistic means of supporting students. Additionally, a lead teacher and counselor augmented teacher and student support, respectively. The belief in the teaming model, as well as our program anchors, was based upon research illuminating the fact that school structures that offer "personalization for academic and social learning" remain among the best means for ensuring student and school success.

Next was our approach to content-specific common planning. While the teams were cross-curricular in nature, the master schedule allowed content area colleagues planning during the same block of time. This common content area planning was used to co-plan lessons, share best practices, analyze assessment data, and to discuss interventions. As a result, teachers were supported by their cross-curricular teammates as well as their content area peers.

Our approach to professional learning ensured the sound implementation of each of the program's anchors. A lead teacher was charged with organizing and setting the agenda for the teams' bi-weekly professional learning team (PLT) meetings. These meetings provided ongoing staff development aimed at fully supporting team members' efforts to achieve program goals. Informal observations conducted by the lead teacher and videotaped lesson studies were key aspects of each team's professional learning and helped frame the collaborative dialogue in the PLT meetings. Assessing student work and organizing extension and experiential learning activities were also PLT agenda items.

PROGRAM ANCHORS

ACADEMIC

Academic Goal One: *Improve student note-taking skills*

For this goal, the team selected the Cornell note-taking method. This method was chosen because it aligns with College Board strategies for success in Advanced Placement courses, and it provides a structure that encourages the selection, paraphrasing, and summary of information from a variety of sources. This goal is broken down into three indicators, with the first being the introduction and review of the Cornell note-taking style in content classes. After expectations for note-taking are understood, the second indicator moves teachers into assigning note-taking in class. The third indicator focuses on the team's review of student note-taking samples. Mastering this skill not only aids students with synthesizing information, but it also prepares students for higher-level texts in which subheadings or other supportive text features are not provided. Note-taking is key to aiding students with organizing and understanding content.

Academic Goal Two: *Improve student organization skills*

Effective time-management and organizational skills are critical for success in high school and beyond. The ACE program provided every student with a binder, dividers, and agenda planning book. This uniformity of materials not only increases access to success for all students, but it also standardizes expectations and organization in the classroom. The three indicators the team used for the development of this goal included the dissemination of materials, the setting up of the binders as directed by teachers in accordance with program expectations, and consistent binder checks were held to ensure students remained organized. The use of agenda books was required and helped students chart assignments, grades, and pertinent school information. When students produced a thoroughly completed agenda book and well-organized binder for a given period of time, prizes and gift certificates were awarded.

Academic Goal Three: *Improve student reflection and discussion skills*

The ACE team employed Socratic seminars and student-led tutorials as common instructional strategies to meet this goal. The Socratic seminar was selected for use in social studies, science, and English, while student-led tutorials were used in mathematics. Both strategies teach students how to reflect on their learning and to solicit questions. Both strategies provided important leadership opportunities for students as they grow into mature thinkers and learners. In the Socratic seminar, students were engaged not only in the formation of discussion topics but also in reviewing the process itself. This review encouraged reflection on what makes academic discourse successful through the analysis of the speaking and listening skills needed to contribute positively to a discussion. One of the most successful methods used to improve instruction in this area was the use of video in team meetings. Teachers were recorded conducting the seminars and tutorials in their classrooms. These videos were then reviewed during team meetings and served as a means to drive improvement in this goal area.

Academic Goal Four: *Develop independent argumentative and expository writing skills*

The indicators within this goal focused students on the composition of a high school level thesis statement, the identification of appropriate source-based evidence, the construction of structurally sound and coherent sentences, and the use of the outlining and revision processes. To support student growth in these areas, the team reviewed students' writing samples to identify areas of strengths and weaknesses. Appropriate team-based interventions were then created to address areas of concern. In addition, students used a variety of review processes to gain additional feedback on their writing. For example, in English class, students worked with senior-level students to review drafts of their writing and gain feedback. On another writing assignment, teachers from the English department, as well as other content areas, read and provided feedback on ninth-grade students' drafts. In this case, the feedback was given through a student-led conference, and students were offered a series of revision opportunities.

Academic Goal Five: *Develop independent and sustained reading skills*

The indicators for this goal focused on the use of before, during, and after reading strategies in the classrooms, as well as the assessment of reading across content areas. Student success on these reading assessments were reviewed by the team to identify strengths and weaknesses. Targeted team-wide interventions to address this goal included the use of prediction as a before reading strategy. This strategy is one that can be embraced by all four content areas and thus more easily reinforced during instruction. For example, in math class, the teacher infused prediction in word problems. In English class, this same strategy was used to discuss possible plot lines. While in science class, students used prediction before lab experiments as a part of the overall scientific method. Prediction as a before reading strategy reinforces the mental process of engaging with and preparing to digest new information.

Included in the ACE during reading strategies was the use of silent, independent, and sustained reading to build stamina. Implemented alongside the Cornell note-taking system, this expectation provided students with the opportunity to engage with text individually for 20 minutes of uninterrupted time. While at times this is extended (especially in English classes), the team agreed that 20 minutes was an appropriate amount of time to allow students to work independently with new text before returning to more collaborative instructional strategies. As students move into college and the workforce they must be able to read well independently.

When breaking down text after reading, the team used common graphic organizers for outlining arguments. Before submitting this outline, students conducted peer reviews and held discussions about the quality and depth of evidence. Students were required to use direct quotes from the text as evidence and to provide subsequent explanations of how those quotes were directly connected to the students' theses. This practice encouraged reflection on the appropriate selection of evidence, as well as its meaning and relationship to the thesis. Overall, it helped students improve their ability to synthesize ideas in their argumentative writing.

CHARACTER

Character Strengths Goal Six: *Develop student resilience and academic commitment via character strength development*

During the first week of school, students across the ninth grade took part in a lesson that introduced them to four character strengths that served as the foundation of the ACE program: a) persistence, b) social intelligence, c) kindness, and d) citizenship. These strengths were described as the commitment to being engaged with complex challenges, being a positive and supportive member of large and small groups, seeking out ways to acknowledge the contributions made by others, and working toward the betterment of the school and the local community. The indicators of the ACE character development goal were for teachers and students to be aware of these strengths, be reflective of how they influence well-being and confidence, and help with creating thoughtful plans for growth. Throughout the year, students were given opportunities to reflect upon and celebrate their strengths.

Weekly announcements were presented to ninth grade classes which recognized positive examples of students who exhibited the identified character strengths. In addition to the weekly recognition of these strengths, quarterly reflections were conducted. During these times, students reflected on their character strength goals for the quarter, ranked their current character strength development, and conducted student-led conferences. Students created the notes for their conferences by identifying examples of their strengths from the prior quarter. Students identified their most underdeveloped areas, and then they composed "if-then" statements identifying the impact the areas may have on their confidence and well-being. The conference closed with the students identifying goals for the upcoming quarter, their prediction of challenges they might encounter, and ways that they were going to address those challenges. It is important to note that the teacher who was listening to these student-led conferences played an important role as a sounding board – but not as a critical reviewer. They were supportive of the student's reflection and provided only positive feedback on the growth that was identified by the student.

EXTENSION

Extension Goal Seven: *Ensure that students are fully aware of their post-secondary options and "think beyond" their own communities*

Maximizing students' opportunities in high school includes establishing a clear understanding of post-secondary school goals. The extension section of the ACE program focused on having students develop a "post-high school self-image" during their ninth-grade year. While they may not necessarily have a specific major or career goal in mind, they needed an understanding of the expectations for and benefits of a variety of career clusters. "Frontloading" these conversations in the ninth grade supported more informed decision making throughout the high school experience. To help students create a post-high school self-image, the ninth graders visited two college campuses (4-year and 2-year colleges), conducted college and career readiness evaluations using the Naviance program, and participated in a "Career Day" lesson with representatives from local businesses.

Each of the college visits was distinguished by clear "look-fors" and well-planned activities to ensure students became familiar with the extensive nature of college. These activities included partnering with the colleges to ensure students had access to admissions counselors as well as student panels during these visits. Further, specific activities included "campus investigations," campus tours, attending lecture-style classes, and visiting dorm rooms and student unions. Students also completed reflection activities upon their return from the trip, which furthered their understanding.

The ninth grade counselor used the Naviance program to help students identify career clusters that aligned with their skills and interests, as well as provided resources for college and career readiness. More specifically, the program was used as a means to help students track their GPA, research college admissions criteria, and take a series of interest surveys. The survey results suggested career clusters the students may have wanted to consider as they set post-high school goals. Students used the combined results of that survey with the college tours to identify a cluster they wanted to learn more about during the Ninth Grade Career Day. Students were then grouped by clusters and created questions that they used to engage in informed discussions with members of the local business community. Providing this type of information to ninth graders aids their decision making and broadens their awareness of important career requirements, and it helps them make the connection between high school and life thereafter. Figure 8 illustrates the ACE plan.

Simple. Practical. Effective.

Figure 8: **ACE Action Plan**

Ninth Grade ACE Program

The Ninth Grade ACE Program will maximize student potential at ABC High School by providing instruction and support in the development of academic skills, character strengths, and post high school planning.

	Goal 1: Improve Student Note-Taking Skills	**Action/Strategy**	**Person(s) Responsible**	**Date**
A C A D E M I C	Indicator 1.1	Introduce the Cornell note-taking system to ninth grade students	Government Teachers	August-September
	Indicator 1.2	Assign reading and Cornell notes for gathering information in class	Ninth Grade Team Members	Daily
	Indicator 1.3	Review student work samples of Cornell notes in Ninth Grade Professional Learning Team (PLT) in order to identify anchor papers, develop consistent grading practices, and target common strengths and weaknesses	Ninth Grade Professional Learning Team	September
	Goal 2: Improve Student Organization Skills	**Action/Strategy**	**Person(s) Responsible**	**Date**
	Indicator 2.1	Provide binders and dividers with a common organization for every incoming ninth grade student	Ninth Grade Team Members	August

ACADEMIC

	Action/Strategy	Person(s) Responsible	Date
Indicator 2.2	Reinforce use of binders during warm-up/drill and wrap up of every core academic class	Ninth Grade Team Members	Daily
Indicator 2.3	Reinforce organization with daily use of student agenda for homework, organization, and planning	Ninth Grade Team Members	Daily
Indicator 2.4	Conduct quarterly binder checks using the abbreviated "AVID-like" rubric for assessment. Prior to these checks, students will be given the opportunity to review their organization during coach class	Ninth Grade Team Members	Quarterly
Indicator 2.5	Provide a calendar of weekly opportunities for students to attend a coach class for additional support in each academic subject	Guidance/Ninth Grade Team	August
Goal 3: Improve Student Skills in Reflection and	**Action/Strategy**	**Person(s) Responsible**	**Date**
Indicator 3.1	Introduce Socratic seminar to classes	English/Government Teachers	September
Indicator 3.2	Introduce Student-Led Tutorials to classes	Math Teachers	Second Quarter
Indicator 3.3	Integration of one Socratic Seminar or Student-Led Tutorials	Ninth Grade Team Members	Quarterly, beginning in the second quarter

Simple. Practical. Effective.

	Goal 4: Develop Independent Argumentative and Expository Writing Skills	Action/Strategy	Person(s) Responsible	Date
ACADEMIC	Indicator 4.1	Introduce thesis statement composition, including a claim and three logical reasons	English and Government Teachers	Second Quarter
	Indicator 4.2	Introduce the selection of content specific supporting evidence	English and Government Teachers	Second Quarter
	Indicator 4.3	Provide written assessments which require expository and/or argumentative writing, including full thesis development	English and Government Teachers	Third and Fourth Quarter
	Indicator 4.4	Review student writing samples during Professional Learning Team (PLT) meetings in order to identify anchor papers, develop consistent grading practices, and target common strengths and weaknesses	Ninth Grade Professional Learning Team	Quarterly
	Indicator 4.5	Peer review and extended argumentative and/or expository writing samples with senior-level students	English Teachers	Fourth Quarter

	Goal 5: Develop Independent and Sustained Reading Skills in Informative and Narrative Text	Action/Strategy	Person(s) Responsible	Date
ACADEMIC	Indicator 5.1	Provide before, during, and after reading instruction with a variety of informative and narrative texts which provide students with opportunities to read silently and independently for at least 20 minutes	English, Government, and/or Science Teachers	Weekly
	Indicator 5.2	Provide professional development on the differentiated Lexile levels in order to target individual student reading levels	Ninth Grade Professional Learning Team	October
	Indicator 5.3	Review content reading assessments during Professional Learning Team (PLT) meetings in order to identify anchor papers, develop consistent grading practices, and target common strengths and weaknesses	Ninth Grade Professional Learning Team	Quarterly

Simple. Practical. Effective.

	Goal 6: Develop Student Resilience and Academic Commitment via Character Strength Development	Action/Strategy	Person(s) Responsible	Date
C H A R A C T E R	Indicator 6.1	Review the definitions and applications of the four-character strengths (kindness, citizenship, persistence, and social intelligence)	Ninth Grade Team Members	August
	Indicator 6.2	Introduce the use of character strengths in school to ninth grade students	English Teachers	First Week of School
	Indicator 6.3	Provide visual reminders for the character strengths by hanging posters of the identified strengths in every ninth-grade classroom	Ninth Grade Team Members	September
	Indicator 6.4	Reinforce the identification of the development of character strengths with an affirmation of students' use of strengths during class, acknowledging achievements on the "Shout Out" board, weekly announcements, and parent phone calls home	Teachers and Students on the Ninth Grade Team	Daily

C H A R A C T E R	Indicator 6.5	Identification and review areas of growth using the character strength reflection chart and student-led conferencing	Ninth Grade Students/ English Teachers	Quarterly
	Indicator 6.6	Review of character strengths and growth areas through self-reflection using the Naviance program	Guidance	Quarterly
	Indicator 6.7	Develop pride and citizenship in the school community by expanding the relationships with feeder elementary schools to increase student volunteer opportunities	Ninth Grade Team and Students	First and Second Semester
	Indicator 6.8	Present student workshops "AVID's What I Would Tell My Ninth Grade Self" to all ninth-grade classes	Ninth Grade Team, Selected Upperclassmen, Tenth Grade Student Representatives, 12th Grade AVID teacher.	First Quarter
	Indicator 6.9	Conduct a diagnostic social-emotional assessment to determine the needs for small group counseling to be held throughout the year	Guidance, Ninth Grade Students	First Quarter
	Indicator 6.10	Review annual progress and smooth the transition into 10th grade by conducting an end of year assembly focusing on strengths gained throughout the year	Ninth Grade Students, Guidance	Fourth Quarter

	Goal 7: Improve Long Term Planning for Post High School Experience	Action/Strategy	Person(s) Responsible	Date
EXTENSION	Indicator 7.1	Establish an understanding of the requirements and realities of the college experience by visiting two local colleges and conducting virtual college tours.	Guidance	Second and Third Quarter
	Indicator 7.2	Track college readiness and preparedness using the Naviance program	Guidance	January
	Indicator 7.3	Provide opportunities for students to interact with members of a variety of careers in a spring career day fair	Guidance	Fourth Quarter
	Indicator 7.4	Weekly in-class announcements to include school information, community opportunities, and weekly shout-outs	Team Leader, Guidance	Weekly
	Indicator 7.5	Provide parent support for the post-high school experience through information sessions on support services and college planning	Team Leader, Guidance	Quarterly

Benefits of ACE

The combination of academics, character strengths, and extension was what made this program unique. Providing this multi-faceted foundation during ninth grade supports students' development while easing their transition into high school. With the implementation of this program, our school witnessed improvement in academic outcomes and overall school climate. Without question, the ACE program provided the underpinning for the school's improvements. The ACE program was recognized on the state level for its focus on character development. In addition to the improved outcomes and external acknowledgment of the program, students, too, sounded off in support of the program's usefulness. Student survey data gleaned that 85% of 9th grade students believed their behavior and work ethic had improved, 80% noted they were much more informed of college and career options, and 90% found the academic skills taught in the program to be useful in better preparing them for high school and college. With this program in place, the foundation was set for the school to attain notable improvements in the areas of AP exam scores, SAT performance, and graduation rate.

CHAPTER 8

The College Metrics

An Action Plan for Setting Students Up for Success on College Metrics

As discussed, with the technological/information age came a dramatically increased need for education beyond high school. Compounding the need for schooling beyond secondary education is the sharp proliferation in the competitive nature of our world's global economy. In essence, the economic shifts we have experienced as a result of the technological/information age have forced the amelioration of many good-paying, labor-oriented jobs and moved those jobs into sectors requiring college degrees and other forms of post-secondary training (Wagner, 2008). At the same time, more and more members of the international community are seeking employment here in the United States or working for American companies that have outsourced "information age type jobs" (jobs often requiring college degrees) overseas. As such, now more so than ever, there is a profound need for students to leave high school with the skills and knowledge necessary to complete college as a means to compete for good-paying jobs. Unfortunately, however, the need for better college preparation has eluded far too many of America's students, especially those in our low-income school communities. Thus, we are witnessing the proverbial "Matthew effect" wherein the poor truly continue to get poorer, and millions of low-income students and families of all races are systematically being left behind with little to no hope for the social mobility that is believed to be the cornerstone of the "American Dream."

In no uncertain terms, there has never been a greater need for a call to action to ensure students are graduating high school truly ready for college and today's technological/information age jobs. Student performance on the SAT, as well as participation and success in the AP program, while not the only measures, are key markers for gauging student readiness as it relates to college-level work. Knowing this, the leadership team and I worked to develop strategies and action plans that would maximize our students' performance on these important measures.

SAT:

The SAT continues to be a consistent and objective measure of college readiness, and its importance has increased significantly in the past several years as more school districts adopt "Junior SAT Day" as a means to offer equity by increasing access. In these instances, schools can no longer inflate SAT scores by "siphoning the top" and only allowing those believed to be the best and brightest to sit for the SAT. Now a school's scores on the SAT are a reflection of the aggregate school performance and, thus, is a good means to set goals and to track and monitor student learning. Further, the fact that Junior SAT Day traditionally takes place at the end of junior year and focuses on critical reading, writing, and mathematics skills makes it a worthy goal on which most staff can have an impact.

Consequently, the first strategy undertaken by our school staff was to ensure that one of all teachers' student learning objectives (SLOs) was connected directly to argumentative writing. All staff, using their respective content topics, agreed to focus their student learning objectives (SLO), the "quantitative measure" used in the teacher evaluation system, on argumentative writing. We chose this approach because argumentative prose requires the ability to research, weigh evidence, organize writing in a coherent manner, present cogent facts, and understand varying perspectives by addressing counterclaims. Additionally, this strategy meshed with our school-wide PLT focus on writing. If you recall, this process and our rationale were detailed in Chapter 3. Implicit in one's ability to craft a sound argumentative essay is the ability to read multiple sources and to take copious notes on the varying perspectives. Thus, this focus on argumentative writing buttressed the need for and importance of reading and annotating. Again, this aided in our efforts to make sure we were working in a systemic fashion to improve school-wide achievement in the area of literacy, which would bear a positive impact on student learning as measured by SAT performance. Of course, a focus on argumentative writing also had a residual impact on just about every measure of student performance, including success in the AP program.

More targeted and specific strategies to improve SAT performance started first with counseling all students in grades 10 and 11 to take the PSAT. By doing so and by carefully analyzing the Summary of Answers and Skills (SOAS) report, we were able to identify students' specific needs and strengths in mathematics and in critical reading. This information, when used correctly, is invaluable in gauging student abilities and ensuring student growth. Using the information gleaned from this report, we were able to develop the appropriate support structures which, in addition to our SAT prep course, included our during and after school "SAT Blast" sessions as well as our weekend "SAT Tutorials." Students' grade 10 PSAT scores were used to determine which students would be best served to participate in our grade 11 SAT prep course; these scores were then used to help students assess the areas in which they could improve the most. In essence, at the beginning of the SAT prep course, students created an individual learning plan that was later updated based on their grade 11 PSAT scores. The SAT prep course was scheduled so students were enrolled in SAT prep math and reading on alternating days for the duration of the school year. Additionally, with the understanding that the school's focus on literacy would have a limited direct impact on improving SAT math scores, the math department implemented daily SAT drills in all sophomore and junior classes. While these drills spiraled through the four main areas of SAT math, importance was placed on ensuring students had the most exposure to algebra and functions related questions since those questions comprised the largest portion of the SAT math section.

Our SAT Blast sessions were open access to all upper-classmen and were run several days a week through the school's advisory block and during the school's afternoon coach class sessions. These sessions allowed students to get additional support in mathematics and critical reading and focused on more than test-taking strategies. Similar to our SAT prep course, teachers would assist students in reviewing their SOAS report and help the students determine which topics and concepts they would focus on during these sessions. During these sessions, students were placed into groups based on their needs and worked collaboratively with their peers and the teacher to improve their learning. As you will see in our SAT/PSAT Action Plan (Figure 9), these sessions ran throughout the year to ensure support for seniors and juniors taking the SAT. To further support senior year SAT improvement and to help select junior students improve their chances of achieving recognition by the National Merit Scholarship or National Achievement Scholarship programs, the school designed and offered a series of "SAT Summer Institutes" which, like all of our supports, was free of charge for our students. Please note that our school's literacy focus and strategies were deeply ingrained in all these SAT/PSAT support offerings; hence, this is why the first indicator in the plan emphasizes our commitment to quality literacy-focused instruction across the content areas. We fully understood that literacy remained the most valuable method to yield positive changes in student learning. Shown in the SAT/PSAT Action Plan (Figure 9) is a list of strategies that schools can implement to support student performance on the SAT and PSAT.

*Figure 9: **SAT/PSAT Action Plan***

ABC High School – SAT/PSAT ACTION PLAN

Goal: Improve SAT Performance	Action/Strategy	Person(s) Responsible	Date
Indicator 1.1	Quality first instruction - Reading and writing across content areas	All Staff	Ongoing
Indicator 1.2	Require School-wide SLO to focus on argumentative writing	All Staff	Aug-Feb
Indicator 1.3	Require two *Algebra/Functions mini lessons/warm-ups per week in Junior level math courses: Alg. II, Trig w/Alg., Honors Pre-Calc, & AP Stats	Math Dept.	Aug-June
Indicator 1.4	Analyze Junior SOAS report and use data to plan October and November SAT Blast sessions for seniors	Admin/ English and Math Chairs	Summer
Indicator 1.5	Require ALL 9th, 10th, and 11th graders to take the PSAT	Guidance	Oct.

Indicator 1.6	Offer select 12th and 11th grade students (those 11th graders approaching the NMSQT and NAS index scores as sophomores) opportunities to participate in Sept/October SAT Blast sessions in preparation for Nov SAT (12th graders) and Oct PSAT (11th graders)	Admin/ Guidance/ English and Math Chairs	Sept-Oct
Indicator 1.7	Use Sophomore SOAS / PSAT scores to strategically schedule a Jr. SAT prep course for rising juniors (number of sections TBD). Use Khan Academy to supplement SAT Prep courses and SAT Blast sessions with differentiated, targeted instruction.	Admin/ Guidance	Jan-March
Indicator 1.8	Increase junior year AP participation to ensure that juniors are exposed to rigorous content prior to taking the SAT.	Admin/ Guidance	Jan-March
Indicator 1.9	Ensure that all students who take the PSAT attend a score review session during school hours	Guidance/ English Teachers	Jan
Indicator 1.10	Establish a partnership with an outside vendor to offer weekend SAT prep sessions to identified junior students based on PSAT performance.	Admin/ Guidance/ Math and English Chairs	Feb-March
Indicator 1.11	SAT information session and test-taking strategies presented to juniors prior to SAT Day	Guidance/ English Teachers	March-April

Indicator 1.12	Offer two weeks of SAT Blast Sessions in ALL Grade 11 ELA classes (45 min sessions)	English Teachers	March-April
Indicator 1.13	Plan and implement SAT Summer Institute for rising seniors	Math and English Chairs	May-Aug

Advanced Placement (AP):

Like the SAT, success on AP exams provides a consistent measure of college readiness. Further, these exams provide opportunities for students to earn college credit while in high school, which, in turn, can save students thousands of dollars. Understanding this, we also made participation and success in the AP program a school goal. To improve AP performance, we started first by forming an AP committee that included all of the school's AP and Honors level teachers, the school's staff development teacher, and myself as the principal. The committee determined that it would take a two-pronged approach to improve performance; the first prong would focus on consistent quality instruction in AP courses, and the second prong centered on improving the school's AP culture.

The first action taken to improve AP instruction was to ensure that all AP and Honors level teachers received the training necessary to fully understand AP content and curricula. Therefore, the school paid for these teachers to attend one of the more reputable AP Institutes, sponsored by the CollegeBoard, each summer. In essence, if one was to teach AP level courses at our school, then the expectation was he or she would attend this training prior to teaching the course and then again a year or two after gaining experience teaching the course. The committee also enacted monthly meetings where the focus was on sharing best practices related to:

1. Effective writing instruction,
2. Reviewing and analyzing student responses to course specific free-response questions,
3. Discussing how each teacher was aligning her or his classroom assignments and assessments to best emulate exam content, and
4. Developing the schedule and content for the quarterly AP Boot Camps, which focused on AP skill building in the areas of studying, time

management, sustained independent reading, note-taking, crafting sound essays, and a host of other skills deemed important for success in any AP course.

The committee also applied for and successfully procured a grant that was used for purchasing supplemental teacher and student course materials. The monies were also used to fund after school and weekend AP tutorials for students struggling to master the very complex and dense course material. Teachers used multiple sources of student data to project exam scores for each of their students and were challenged to examine how closely their quarter grades mirrored student projected success on the pending AP exam. This practice was essential to ensuring our grades were not inflated and that the grades were comported with student readiness for the key outcome's assessment, which was the AP exam. Just as importantly, though, teachers were required to determine what was needed to support those students who were not projected to be successful on the exam. This type of reflection and discussion helped teachers develop an understanding of student needs as they related directly to student success in the course. The school also purchased software that afforded students access to hundreds of AP multiple-choice questions; this software was used to provide quiz and unit exam review and provided teachers with student outcome data aligned to course content and topics broken down by unit.

To improve AP culture and to build a more inclusive program, we began using AP potential as means to ensure that students with the ability to find success in the AP program were encouraged to take AP courses. Teachers were also encouraged to recommend students based on work ethic and ability regardless of whether they were identified in the AP potential process. This process further ensured inclusivity and gave voice to the teachers who knew and understood students' abilities the best. Counselors worked closely with students aspiring to attend four-year colleges to strongly encourage them to take at least one AP course prior to graduation. All students identified by AP potential and/or via teacher recommendations were invited to an AP Fair. Similar to a college fair, the AP Fair took place prior to the course registration process and afforded students the chance to explore and learn about each of the school's AP offerings. Each AP teacher showcased her or his course by way of brochures, videos, presentations, and other forms of media designed to pique student interest. To make the AP experience desirable and to provide a level of support, the school held AP orientations, AP socials, AP Boot Camps, provided students with AP jerseys, and sponsored annual $1,000 student scholarships awarded based on student enrollment and success in AP courses.

Shown in Figure 10 is the Advanced Placement Action Plan used to increase access to the AP program as well as bolster improvement in our outcomes.

*Figure 10: **Advanced Placement Action Plan***

ABC High School – ADVANCED PLACEMENT ACTION PLAN

Goal 1: Improve Performance in the Advanced Placement Program	Action/Strategy	Person(s) Responsible	Date
Indicator 1.1	Extend opportunities for AP teachers as well as prospective AP and Honors level teachers to attend the Summer AP Institute. This will help support our continued efforts to build AP vertical teaming.	Admin	July
Indicator 1.2	Establish and follow AP Quarterly Exam & Quiz Schedule ; teacher-created assessments must be clearly aligned to AP exams (multiple choice and free response questions)	AP Teachers/ Admin	Nov/Jan/ April
Indicator 1.3	Use of private software as a "Test Items Bank" to help develop teacher-created assessments that align with AP expectations and format	AP Teachers	Ongoing
Indicator 1.4	Use online tutorials (i.e., Edmodo) to extend classroom lessons	AP Teachers	Ongoing

Indicator 1.5	Provide after school AP Coach Classes based on unit assessment results (minimum of 3 per quarter)	AP Teachers/ Admin	Quarterly
Indicator 1.6	Hold monthly AP teacher meetings to discuss challenges and concerns in an effort to improve AP level instruction and student performance *Topics to include: a) analysis of AP Instructional Planning Reports, b) review of unit assessment and quiz data, c) sharing of FRQ/writing samples, d) best practices for using private software/test items bank (i.e., presentation of sample questions), e) updates on after school coach classes and f) planning AP events*	AP Teachers	Monthly
Indicator 1.7	Create a standard for reading (i.e., required pre-reading strategies with accompanying Cornell notes as well as timed readings with follow up comprehension questions) Create a standard for writing assignments in AP courses - In class writing assignments must be based on prior AP exam release prompt and scoring rubric	AP Teachers	Monthly
Indicator 1.8	Ensure that the student scheduling provides optimal opportunities for students to enroll in one or more AP courses and make efforts to keep AP classes under 18 students (when possible)	Guidance/ Admin/Chairs	Ongoing

Indicator 1.9	Hold an end of year AP Orientation to provide students with course overviews, outlines, and summer assignments	AP Teachers/ Guidance	June
Indicator 1.10	Create course options that provide for vertical teaming and or additional AP strategies (development of strong reading and writing skills). Options could include: *double block of select AP courses and or a .5 credit Career Strategies/ AP support course*	Admin	Ongoing
Goal 2: Promote the Importance of and Market student success in the AP Program.	**Action/Strategy**	**Person(s) Responsible**	**Date**
Indicator 2.1	Use of AP Potential to identify students capable of AP coursework	Guidance/ Admin	Dec/Jan
Indicator 2.2	Talk to AP classes about the importance/benefits of taking AP exams	AP Teachers/ Guidance	August
Indicator 2.3	Hold AP Fair to promote the benefits of AP courses and to ensure an inclusive program	AP Teachers/ Guidance	Jan
Indicator 2.4	Provide a financial incentive structure/discounted rates and other incentives for students who register for multiple exams	Guidance/ Admin	Jan-March
Indicator 2.5	Hold Annual AP Day and AP Night to promote student and community awareness of the benefits of the AP program	AP Teachers/ Guidance/ Admin/Chairs	Jan/Feb

Indicator 2.6	Develop the AP Student of the Year Award to be given to a senior based on the recommendations of the AP Committee	AP Teachers/ Admin	May
Indicator 2.7	Hold Quarterly AP Boot Camps/ Socials/Luncheons for students enrolled in AP courses to reward academic excellence and build a strong AP Culture	AP Teachers/ Guidance	Nov/Jan/ April
Indicator 2.8	Promote the AP Program as a means to improve SAT performance and college success	AP Teachers/ Guidance/ Admin	Ongoing
Indicator 2.9	AP Course Audit to CollegeBoard	AP Coordinator/ Guidance	May
Indicator 2.10	AP Orientation session for the upcoming school year	AP Teachers	June

After a few years of implementation, our school's College Metrics Action Plans proved effective. Average scores on the SAT increased by 40 points, and there was a doubling in the number of students meeting the CollegeBoard's College Readiness Indicator on the SAT. With regards to the AP program, there was a 50% increase in AP participation with a 5% increase in the percent of students achieving a qualifying exam score of three or higher, and we nearly doubled our Equity and Excellence (E&E) rate. These data points improved the amount of academic scholarship money awarded to our students. More specifically, the amount of scholarship money awarded more than doubled as a result of these action plans.

CHAPTER 9

Fulfilling the "Promise of Preparation"

Graduation Action Plan:

Critics of graduation rates as a means to gauge college and workforce readiness often cite the wide variation between graduation requirements from system to system and state to state. Furthermore, these critics also purport that what is required to successfully complete a high school program of study can range dramatically from one school to the next. In all honesty, these claims do bear some degree of merit. With that being said, borrowing the words of a former supervisor of mine, I framed our efforts to improve our graduation on the idea of a "promise of preparation." This promise of preparation entailed ensuring students did not simply graduate on time; a high school diploma needs to certify more than seat time and compliance. Rather, we sought to assure that our students left high school with the literacy competencies necessary to be successful in life and so they could employ those literacy skills to become well-informed citizens capable of fully participating in the democratic process. Our school subscribed to the belief that "literacy is the real social justice" and is the single most important factor in "leveling the playing field" in college and in the workforce. Hence, as noted repeatedly throughout this book, everything we did as a staff was based on this promise of preparation by way of our energies to fully immerse students in literacy. The efforts detailed in our ACE, AP, and SAT/PSAT Action Plans were means for ensuring we fulfilled our promise of preparation to every student who we certified as a graduate. Anything less would be akin to a "dereliction of duty." Thus, we were steadfastly committed to providing the academic skills, guidance, and supports to help students graduate on time and fully actualize this promise of preparation. What follows next is a plan that augmented these efforts by providing additional support and progress monitoring of our upper-class students.

As high school principals know, any school will have subsets of students who simply, for a wide range of reasons, need additional support to meet academic expectations and to persist to on-time graduation. This is particularly true in schools that serve low-income communities. So, while a sound instructional program grounded in literacy serves as the foundation for the preparation of promise, it alone does not account for the mentoring, guidance, and progress monitoring necessary to keep students on track. Knowing this, our school leadership team developed a multi-tiered progress monitoring process and an accompanying mentoring program aimed at providing students with differentiated supports. Rising senior and junior classes were organized into five tiers using credits earned and status on state assessments as predictors of on-time graduation. Students were then carefully placed into one of the five tiers representing the likelihood of on-time graduation. These tiers were as follows: a) very high, b) high, c) moderate, d) low moderate, and e) at risk.

Understanding that the best predictor of future performance is past performance, the supports and interventions intensified for those students whose likelihood of graduating on time placed them in the moderate, low-moderate, and at-risk tiers. Our main priority was to "tease out" those students who needed the most support and to intercede with those supports early and often. To that end, students in the at-risk and low moderate tiers were offered weekend, summer, and after school credit recovery options, assigned a staff mentor, and were placed on bi-weekly progress monitoring with the school counselors who reviewed their academic progress to ensure the students fully understood their academic standing in all classes. Staff mentors, each assigned a small group of mentees, frequently reviewed students' grades and attendance and worked with the students' teachers and parents to ensure there were collaborative efforts to support student success. Parents of students not meeting with success at the interim and/or end of quarter marks were required (strongly encouraged) to attend a conference between the student, counselor, mentor, and a member of the administrative team to set clear goals and expectations for how the student would earn the grades, in the succeeding marking periods, to receive the course credit. Students assigned to the moderate tier received similar supports with the exception of the credit recovery options since all of the courses required for graduation could fit into their standard schedule. These supports addressed student progress in their coursework.

As noted, the other factor that often inhibits on-time graduation is student status with regards to state assessment requirements. Naturally, as we improved our literacy-focused instruction, our pass rates on state assessments evidenced a sharp incline. Yet and still, there were and will most certainly always be students who fail to demonstrate their knowledge on standardized assessments. As such, there was a need for identifying and supporting these students in an effort to help them overcome this barrier. Students who were off track for on-time graduation as a result of state assessments were required to attend in-school or after-school intervention sessions geared toward reviewing key standards and topics that were germane to passing the state assessments. Students received standards-based small group instruction and were assessed regularly to determine to what extent they were mastering the state exam's assessment limits. Given that there were multiple assessments required for graduation, sessions rotated days to ensure students needing to pass multiple assessments were able to attend. These sessions ran six to eight weeks prior to the assessment, and student failure to attend was promptly communicated with parents, and the school reserved the right to restrict student participation in extra-curricular and other school activities. While being punitive is never ideal, we needed students and parents to understand the value of taking full advantage of these sessions.

As you know, affecting improvement in student achievement at any school, especially a high school, can seem overwhelming. As a school, we found a tiered and targeted approach to identifying and supporting students to be essential in improving student achievement irrespective of the metric. Clearly, our approach to supporting students in their efforts to graduate on time and actualize the promise of preparation was no exception. Figure 11 is an outline of the tiered support model school staff enlisted to assist upper-class students in their efforts to graduate high school on time.

Figure 11: **Graduation Action Plan (Senior Cohort)**

Graduation Action Plan - Senior Cohort

The ABC High School Graduation Committee will implement a tiered approach to identifying students' graduation status based on credits earned prior to the beginning of the upcoming school year. When identifying students in need of additional supports, the graduation committee will also evaluate students' status in the areas of State Assessments and Student Service Learning Hours (SSLH). The committee will use a proactive and progressive approach based on progress monitoring: the greater the students' needs, the more support and progress monitoring they will receive.

As of September 30, the senior cohort included approximately 300 students. This number was inclusive of current students, dropouts, current students, dropouts, early graduates, and "hanging transfers" (students who have transferred out of ABC High School but haven't yet been reconciled with their new school enrollment). Transfer students entering ABC High School during the school year will be added to the cohort and provided the appropriate supports based on their entering status. This will ensure proper tracking of students entering and exiting the cohort.

Graduation Committee Members:

- Assistant Principal - Co-chair
- Assistant Principal - Co-chair
- Principal
- Pupil Personnel Worker
- School Counselor - Chair
- School Counselor
- School Counselor
- Special Education - Chair
- Lead Credit Recovery Teacher

The following Five Tier Model has been developed to support students, in the form of progress monitoring, based on their accumulated credits at the beginning of the school year. The state requires a minimum of 21 credits for graduation containing a mix of required, elective, and career completed courses:

COLOR	CREDITS	LIKELIHOOD	SUPPORT/PROGRESS MONITORING	PERSON(S) RESPONSIBLE
GREEN	21 or more	Very High	1. Letters for interim & quarter course failures 2. Semester parent meeting for those students who fail a course, 1st and/or 2nd quarter, required for graduation	1. Admin/Counselors 2. Admin/Counselors
BLUE	18-20.5	High	1. Letters for interim & quarter course failures 2. Semester parent meeting for those students who fail a course, 1st and/or 2nd quarter, required for graduation	1. Admin/Counselors 2. Admin/Counselors

YELLOW	15-17.5	Moderate	1. Proactive "Concern" Meetings – September 2. Letters for interim & quarter course failures 3. Quarter meeting for those students who fail a course, 1st or 2nd quarter, required for graduation 4. Semester parent meeting for those students who fail a course, 1st and/or 2nd quarter, required for graduation 5. For students not meeting with success at the end of quarter 2, progress will be monitored on 2-week cycles 6. Students failing a course after quarter 3 will be provided the option to be graded out/fail the course and begin credit recovery in our weekend and twilight sessions	1. Admin/ Counselors 2. Admin/ Counselors 3. Admin/ Counselors 4. Admin/ Counselors 5. Counselors 6. Admin/ Credit Recovery Team

ORANGE	13-14.5	Low Moderate	1. Proactive "Concern" Meetings – September 2. Assigned a staff mentor 3. Letters for interim & quarter course failures 4. Quarter meeting for those students who fail a course, 1st or 2nd quarter, required for graduation 5. Semester parent meeting for those students who fail a course, 1st and/or 2nd quarter, required for graduation 6. For students not meeting with success at the end of quarter 2, progress will be monitored on 2-week cycles 7. Students failing a course after quarter 3 will be provided the option to be graded out/fail the course and begin credit recovery in our weekend and twilight sessions	1. Admin/ Counselors 2. SOAR Committee Mentors 3. Admin/ Counselors 4. Admin/ Counselors 5. Admin/ Counselors 6. Counselors 7. Admin/ Credit Recovery Team

RED	12 or less	At-Risk	1. Proactive "Concern" Meetings – September 2. Assigned a staff mentor 3. Letters for interim & quarter course failures 4. Quarter meeting for those students who fail a course, 1st or 2nd quarter, required for graduation 5. Semester parent meeting for those students who fail a course, 1st and/or 2nd quarter, required for graduation 6. For students not meeting with success at the end of quarter 2, progress will be monitored on 2-week cycles 7. Students failing a course after quarter 3 will be provided the option to be graded out/fail the course and begin credit recovery in our weekend and twilight sessions	1. Admin/ Counselors 2. SOAR Committee Mentors 3. Admin/ Counselors 4. Admin/ Counselors 5. Admin/ Counselors 6. Counselors 7. Admin/ Credit Recovery Team

SUMMARY

By implementing this plan, the school evidenced a 12% increase in the on-time graduation rate. It is also important to note that the sharp shift to academics by way of a literacy focus improved the school climate, as evidenced by the 20% decrease in student discipline. For these plans to truly be impactful, the principal, as the instructional leader, must be intimately involved in the planning, implementation, and monitoring of these efforts. While I know that this plan is by no means the only solution to the challenges associated with ensuring all students graduate high school on time and are college and career ready, I do believe these strategies can prove helpful in school's efforts to improve student learning and readiness.

PART IV
CONCLUSION

CHAPTER 10

Final Thoughts

Rather than take an inordinate amount of time rehashing the points that have already been made throughout this book, I will opt for brevity in making my final points. School leaders are among the most impactful people in society. Their success or failures have far-reaching consequences that echo for generations. Few other professions offer this level of power in terms of shaping and influencing so many people. As the saying goes, "with great power comes great responsibility." School leaders must acknowledge and wholly "lean into" this responsibility. In doing so, school leaders must first: (a) recognize that the need to improve literacy skills is unparalleled, and (b) understand that failure to place literacy as the heart of student learning is the single biggest mistake one can make as a school leader.

Further, leaders should embrace the Core Four and understand that successful leadership will require a clear purpose, the right people, a well-developed plan, and unwavering persistence. Without question, the school leaders' primary role is to masterfully orchestrate the intersection between these four concepts. While all four are pivotal to success, as effective instructional leadership goes, there is no substitute for a well-developed plan steeped in literacy. Put another way, even the best staff comprised of the "right people" will struggle to overcome the lack of a sound plan borne out of a compelling purpose. The impact of unwavering persistence, too, would be hindered by the lack of such a plan because standing firm behind an ineffective plan might be worse than the absence of one altogether. In light of these points, throughout this book, a great deal of attention was directed to the requisite strategies and thought processes for meaningful school

Simple. Practical. Effective.

improvement. Hopefully, the book has provided a simple, practical, and effective roadmap or compass of sorts that can help you establish or refine your literacy-focused instructional leadership framework.

REFERENCES

Achieve.Org. (, 2020). *Rising challenge survey.* Retrieved from https://www.achieve.org/rising-challenge-survey-2-powerpoint

Alliance for Excellent Education. (2016). *Adolescent Literacy: Bridging the college and career readiness gap.* Washington, DC: Author.

Collins, J. (2001). *Good to great.* Harper Collins.

Colver, G. (2010). *Talent is overrated: What really separates world-class performers from everybody else.* Penguin Group.

Conley, D. T. (2003). *College knowledge: What it takes for students to succeed and what we can do to get them ready.* Jossey-Bass

Dweck, C. (2009). Mindsets: Developing talent through a growth mindset. *Olympic Coach, 21*, 4.

Dweck, C. (2012). *Mindset: How you can fulfill your potential.* New York: Ballantine Books.

Gallagher, K. (2009). Readicide. Portland, ME: Stenhouse Publishers

Hunter, R. (2004). *Madeline Hunter's mastery teaching: Increasing instructional effectiveness in elementary and secondary schools.* Thousand Oaks, CA: Corwin Press

MetLife (2012). The MetLife Survey of the American Teacher: *Challenges for school leadership.* Retrieved from https://www.metlife.com/about-us/newsroom/2013/february/the-metlife-survey-of-the-american-teacher--challenges-for-schoo/#:~:text=for%20School%20Leadership-,The%20MetLife%20Survey%20of%20the%20American%20Teacher%3A%20Challenges%20for%20School,those%20closest%20to%20the%20classroom.

Pink, D. (2009). *Drive: The surprising truth about what motivates us.* Riverhead Books.

Schmoker, M. (2006). *Results now: How we can achieve unprecedented improvements in teaching and learning.* ASCD.

Schmoker, M. (2011). *Focus: Elevating the essentials to radically improve student learning.* ASCD.

U.S. Department of Education, National Center for Education Statistics. (2019). *The Condition of Education 2019* (NCES 2019-144), Undergraduate Retention, and Graduation Rates.

Wagner, T. (2008). Rigor redefined. *Educational Leadership, 66*(2), 20-25.

Whitaker, T. (2012). *What great principals do differently: 18 things that matter most.* Eye On Education.

Whitaker, T. (2018). *Leading school change: How to overcome resistance, increase buy-in, and accomplish your goals* (2nd ed.). Routledge.

ABOUT THE AUTHOR

Dr. Marquis S. Dwarte is a leadership consultant and experienced educator with a proven track record of success as a school principal and district level leader. Dr. Dwarte's two decades of experience span the K-16 continuum and has afforded him principal experience at the elementary, middle, and high school levels. He was the founding principal of an "internationally unique" charter school and an award-winning comprehensive high school principal. As a district-level leader, he has supervised K-12 principals as well as led large-scale system-level initiatives. As an adjunct professor, Dr. Dwarte teaches classes in statistical methods, assessment and evaluation, action research, and quantitative research design. Dr. Dwarte holds a bachelor's degree in sociology from the University of Buffalo (SUNY at Buffalo), a master's degree in counselor education from McDaniel College, and a doctorate in education leadership and social policy from Morgan State University. Dr. Dwarte is published in the areas of college and career readiness, school reform, and minority student achievement.

www.ingramcontent.com/pod-product-compliance
Lightning Source LLC
Chambersburg PA
CBHW081508080526
44589CB00017B/2697